Headlong

Headlong Theatre, Birmingham Repertory Theatre, Liverpool Everyman and Playhouse, Lyric Hammersmith and West Yorkshire Playhouse present

ROUGH CROSSINGS

by Simon Schama
Adapted for the stage by Caryl Phillips

D1059484

LITERATURE AND LANGUAGE DEPARTMENT
THE CHICAGO PUBLIC LIBRARY
400 SOUTH STATE STREET
CHICAGO, ILLINOIS 60605

First performed on 14 September 2007 at Birmingham Repertory Theatre.

R0413928910

Headlong Theatre, Birmingham Repertory Theatre, Liverpool Everyman and Playhouse, Lyric Hammersmith and West Yorkshire Playhouse present

ROUGH CROSSINGS

by Simon Schama
Adapted for the stage by Caryl Phillips

Isaac **Peter Bankole**

Eliza Sharp **Miranda Colchester**

David George **Peter De Jersey**

Johnson / Sergeant Davy / American Officer **Ian Drysdale**

Henry De Mane **Dave Fishley**

Thomas Clarkson **Andy Frame**

William Sharp / Redcoat / Lieutenant **Rob Hastie**

Phyllis George **Dawn Hope**

John Clarkson **Ed Hughes**

Captain / Cornwallis / Falconbridge **Mark Jax**

Ship's Boy / Anna Maria Falconbridge **Jessica Lloyd**

Granville Sharp **Michael Matus**

Sally Peters **Wunmi Mosaku**

James Somerset **Ben Okafor**

Thomas Peters **Patrick Robinson**

Buck Slave / Sierra Leone Settler **Daniel Williams**

All other parts played by members of the company.

Director **Rupert Goold**

Designer **Laura Hopkins**

Lighting Designer **Paul Pyant**

Composer & Sound Designer **Adam Cork**

Video & Projection Designer **Lorna Heavey**

Movement Director **Liz Ranken**

Casting Consultant **Kirsty Kinnear**

Assistant Director **Vik Sivalingam**

Assistant Designer **Simon Kenny**

Production Manager **Spencer New**

Company Stage Manager **Julia Reid**

Deputy Stage Manager **Lucy McMahon**

Assistant Stage Manager **Sarah Jane Davies**

Costume Supervisor **Hilary Lewis**

Re-Lighter & Production Electrician **Tom Snell**

Production Assistant **Jennifer Stowar**

Set Build **Bristol Old Vic**

Production Insurance **Walton and Parkinson**

Press **Clióna Roberts** (0207 704 6224 / cliona@crpr.co.uk)

Production Photography **Manuel Harlan**

Graphic Design **Eureka!**

With thanks to Ian Wainwright (Bristol Old Vic), Jack Bradley,
Clemmie Forfar, Val Cohen, Vinette Robinson, Lucian Msamati,
Paterson Joseph, Angus Wright, Suzann McLean, Victor Power
and

ROUGH CROSSINGS...
WHAT NEXT?

Disclaimer: This should be read after the play has been read or seen.

'Histories never conclude, they just pause their prose. They beat raggedly on into the future...' – Simon Schama

The secret history which this play, and the book upon which it is based, tells is only one of a vast number of smaller stories which together form the terrible narrative of the slave trade. Like all of them, identifying the place where it begins and ends is impossible. Event leads to event and personality influences personality. This play is a fictionalised account of real events. But those real events continued after the period of time dealt with by the play.

After he left Sierra Leone, John Clarkson returned to England, at almost the exact moment that the newly-Republican France declared war on Britain. Clarkson's requests to return to Freetown were ignored by the Sierra Leone Company, as were his brother Thomas' efforts to secure for John the status of Captain which his labours merited. He returned to his hometown of Wisbech. Simon Schama writes that he was being read to, from *The Anti-Slavery Reporter*, when he died there in 1828.

David George returned to Freetown having petitioned the Sierra Leone Company and secured a new Governor for the province, Zachary Macauley. Slowly, in his efforts to maintain order in the settlement, Macauley and his successors eroded the goodwill and the trust of the community who had travelled from Nova Scotia. Petition followed petition and ultimately led to a bloody rebellion, bloodily put down. It was only a matter of time before the idea of independence vanished completely, the Union Jack was raised and in 1808, Freetown officially became part of the British Empire.

Sierra Leone was granted independence by Britain in 1961, but thirty years later the in-fighting and accusations of corruption which had dogged administration after administration erupted into a bloody civil war. Thousands died, and half a million were forced to become refugees. The war ended and elections were held in 2002. The crucial second general election took place as this book was going to print. Sierra Leone now exists as a working, if fragile, democracy.

'Everything that we see is a shadow cast by that which we do not see.'
– Martin Luther King, Jr.

Ben Power
Headlong Literary Associate
August 2007

- c 14,000 – Members of ethnic minority groups living in London in 1775
- 2,143,500 – Members of ethnic minority groups living in London in 2007
- 13,000 – Number of freed Slaves who fought for the defeated British during the American War of Independence
- 1196 – Number of freed slaves who sailed with John Clarkson to found the Province of Freedom in Sierra Leone
- c 50,000 – Number of people who died in the Sierra Leone civil war of the 1990s

SIMON SCHAMA
AUTHOR

 Simon Schama is Professor of History and Art History at Columbia University.

He studied history at Cambridge University where from 1966 to 1976 he was Fellow of Christ's College. From 1976 to 1980 he was Fellow and Tutor in Modern History at Brasenose College, Oxford. From 1980 to 1993 he was Professor of History, Mellon Professor of the Social Sciences and William Kenan Professor of the Humanities at Harvard University and Senior Associate of the Center for European Studies.

He is author of *Patriots and Liberators: Revolution in the Netherlands 1780–1813* (1977) which won the Wolfson Prize for History; *Two Rothschilds and the Land of Israel* (1979); *The Embarrassment of Riches: An Interpretation of Dutch Culture in the Golden Age* (1987); *Citizens. A Chronicle of the French Revolution* (1989) for which he received the major non-fiction prize in the UK, the NCR Prize; the historical novel *Dead Certainties* (1991), now the subject of a PBS film for The American Experience (broadcast in the summer of 2003); *Landscape and Memory* (1995) the winner of the W H Smith Literary Award and the student-voted Lionel Trilling Prize at Columbia; *Rembrandt's Eyes* (1999); the trilogy, *A History of Britain*: volume 1 *The Edge of the World* (2000), volume 2 *The British Wars* (2001) and volume 3 *The Fate of Empire* (2002); *Hang-Ups: Essays on Painting (Mostly)* (2004); *Rough Crossings* (2005), which won the National Book Critics' Circle Prize for Non-fiction; and *The Power of Art* (2007).

Simon Schama has been a regular contributor to *The New Republic*; *The New York Review of Books*; and since 1994, art and cultural critic for *The New Yorker*, winning a National Magazine Award for his art criticism in 1996. He is a regular writer on art and on politics for *The Guardian* and writes on food and cooking for *Vogue*. His criticism has been published in Spanish (2002) as *Confesiones y Encargos*. His books have been translated into fifteen languages. He has received a literature award from the National Academy of Arts and Letters; and in 2001 was made a Commander of the British Empire in the Queen's Birthday Honour List.

His television work as writer and presenter for the BBC includes *Art of the Western World*; *Rembrandt: The Public Gaze and the Private Eye*; a five-part series based on Landscape and Memory; and most recently an award-winning 15-part *History of Britain* which drew four million viewers in the UK and was shown in the United States on the History Channel. His eight-part series *The Power of Art* was broadcast on BBC2 in the autumn of 2006.

CARYL PHILLIPS
PLAYWRIGHT

Caryl Phillips was born in St Kitts and came to Britain at the age of four months. He grew up in Leeds, and studied English Literature at Oxford University.

He began writing for the theatre and his plays include *Strange Fruit* (1980), *Where There is Darkness* (1982) and *The Shelter* (1983). He won the BBC Giles Cooper Award for Best Radio Play of the year with *The Wasted Years* (1984). He has written many dramas and documentaries for radio and television, including, in 1996, the three-hour film of his own novel *The Final Passage*. He wrote the screenplay for the film *Playing Away* (1986) and his screenplay for the Merchant Ivory adaptation of V S Naipaul's *The Mystic Masseur* (2001) won the Silver Ombu for best screenplay at the Mar Del Plata film festival in Argentina.

His novels are: *The Final Passage* (1985), *A State of Independence* (1986), *Higher Ground* (1989), *Cambridge* (1991), *Crossing the River* (1993), *The Nature of Blood* (1997), *A Distant Shore* (2003) and *Dancing in the Dark* (2005). His non-fiction: *The European Tribe* (1987), *The Atlantic Sound* (2000), and *A New World Order* (2001). He is the editor of two anthologies: *Extravagant Strangers: A Literature of Belonging* (1997) and *The Right Set: An Anthology of Writing on Tennis* (1999). His work has been translated into over a dozen languages.

He was named Sunday Times Young Writer of the Year in 1992 and was on the 1993 Granta list of Best of Young British Writers. His literary awards include the Martin Luther King Memorial Prize, a Guggenheim Fellowship, a British Council Fellowship, a Lannan Foundation Fellowship, and Britain's oldest literary award, the James Tait Black Memorial Prize, for *Crossing the River* which was also shortlisted for the 1993 Booker Prize. *A Distant Shore* won the 2004 Commonwealth Writers Prize; *Dancing in the Dark* won the 2006 PEN/Beyond the Margins Award. He is a Fellow of the Royal Society of Literature.

He has taught at universities in Ghana, Sweden, Singapore, Barbados, India, and the United States, and in 1999 was the University of the West Indies Humanities Scholar of the Year. In 2002–3 he was a Fellow at the Centre for Scholars and Writers at the New York Public Library. Formerly Henry R Luce Professor of Migration and Social Order at Columbia University, he is presently Professor of English at Yale University. He is an Honorary Fellow of The Queen's College, Oxford University.

A regular contributor to *The Guardian* and *The New Republic*, his new book *Foreigners* will be published in September 2007 in both Britain and the United States.

www.carylphillips.com

CAST

Peter Bankole
Isaac

Training: Peter trained at Rose Bruford College.
Theatre: *Nakamitsu* (Gate Theatre), *Sing Yer Heart Out for the Lads* (Pilot Theatre Company), *A Midsummer Night's Dream* (RSC Stratford), *The American Pilot* (RSC Soho Theatre), *As You Like It* (RSC Stratford), *Venus & Adonis* (RSC), *A Season of Migration to the North* (RSC).
Television: *The Trial of Gemma Lang, The Bill, The Rotter's Club, Casualty, Doctors*.

Miranda Colchester
Eliza Sharp

Training: Durham University & RADA
Theatre:
Includes *Rock 'n' Roll* (Royal Court/Duke of York's), *The Gunpowder Season* (RSC), *Volpone* (Manchester Royal Exchange), *Summer Lightning* (Northampton Theatre Royal).
Television: Includes *Talk to Me*.
Film: *Churchill at War, The Clap*.
Radio: Includes *'Murder Unprompted'- A Charles Paris Mystery, The Archers, Vongole*.

Peter De Jersey
David George

Training: Central School of Speech and Drama.
Theatre:
Includes *Troilus & Cressida* (National), *Merchant of Venice* (National), *Hamlet* (Cheek by Jowl), *Richard III* (Open Air Theatre), *Macbeth* (US Tour), *Darker Face of Earth* (National), *Someone to Watch Over Me* (Theatr Clwyd), *The Illusion* (Royal Exchange), *A Midsummer Night's Dream* (Open Air Theatre), *King Lear* (RSC), *Kids of Sherwood* (Open Air Theatre), *War & Peace* (National), *Believe What You Will* (RSC), *Sejanus* (RSC), *The Last Days of Don Juan* (RSC), *A New Way to Please You* (RSC), *Troilus & Cressida* (RSC), *The Odyssey* (RSC), *Merry Wives of Windsor* (RSC), *Antony & Cleopatra* (RSC), *As You Like It* (RSC).
Television: *Dalziel & Pascoe, Holby City, Sugar Rush, Urban Gothic, Doctors, Waking the Dead, Trial & Retribution IV, The Bill, Rough Justice, The Choir, New Tricks, Instinct*.
Film: *Out of Depth, Bank Job*.

Ian Drysdale
Johnson / Sergeant Davy / American Officer

Training: Ian trained at Bristol Old Vic Theatre School.

Theatre: Includes *Thomas More, Believe What You Will, Sejanus, Hamlet, Macbeth, The Pilate Project, Brand, Much Ado About Nothing, Antony & Cleopatra* (RSC); *Tear From a Glass Eye* (Gate/National Theatre Studio); *Treasure Island, The Camp* (Tobacco Factory); *Blue Remembered Hills, Knots* (Edinburgh); *The Beaux' Stratagem, Seed of the Bauhinia, A View from the Bridge, Idée Fixe* (Bristol Old Vic); *Deathtrap* (Northern Lights).
TV: Includes *The Verdict, Pulling, The Bill, The English Accent, The South Bank Show* (Shakespeare's Legacy), *Rosie & Jim, Time Gentlemen Please*.
Film: Includes *Size Matters*.
Radio: *Romeo & Juliet*.

Dave Fishley
Henry De Mane

Training: Bristol Old Vic Theatre School.
Theatre: Includes *The Electric Hills* (Liverpool Everyman), *The Odyssey* (Bristol Old Vic/ Lyric Hammersmith), *Macbeth* (Out of Joint/World Tour), *Paradise Lost* (Bristol Old Vic), *A Special Relationship* (York/ National Tour), *Dido, Queen of Carthage* (Shakespeare's Globe), *Caledonian Road* (Almeida Theatre), *Crime and Punishment in Dalston* (Arcola Theatre), *The Nativity* (Young Vic), *Twelfth Night* (Nuffield Southampton), *Eritrea, The Other War* (West Yorkshire Playhouse), *Marat/Sade* (National), *Silverface, Ballad of Wolves* (Gate Theatre), *Now You Know* (Hampstead Theatre), *Asylum! Asylum!* (Abbey Theatre Dublin), *Smoke* (Royal Exchange), *Pop, Jimmy Jazz, The Tempest, Beauty Doesn't Live Here Anymore, Coloured Sands* (Changinspeak).
Television: Includes *Buried* (BAFTA Winner: Best Series), *Casualty, Judge John Deed, A Touch of Frost, Macbeth, The Bill, Between the Lines*.
Film: *Bridget Jones's Diary, If Only, The Fifth Element, Solitaire For Two*.

Andrew Frame
Thomas Clarkson

Training: RADA.
Theatre: Includes *Blue On Blue* (Haymarket Basingstoke), *Market Boy, The Royal Hunt Of The Sun* (National), *Dead Funny* (West Yorkshire Playhouse), *Othello Landscape* (Seinendan, Tokyo), *Festen* (Lyric West End), *The Crucible* (Sheffield Crucible), *All My Sons* (York Theatre Royal), *While I Was Waiting* (BAC), *Marnie* (Haymarket Basingstoke/Gateway Chester), *Romeo & Juliet* (Leicester Haymarket), *Strike*

Gently, Away From Body (Young Vic), *Twelfth Night* (Lyric Belfast), *Small Craft Warnings* (Pleasance London), *She Stoops to Conquer* (Northcott Exeter), *A Passionate Woman, The Tempest* (New Victoria Stoke), *Twelfth Night, Love is a Drug* (Oxford Stage Company), *If We Shadows, L'Ascensore* (Insomniac), *Life On The Planet Surface* (ICA).
Television: Includes *Holby City, EastEnders, Doctors, Murder Prevention, Wire in the Blood, Dreamteam, Trail of Guilt, The Ideal Crush, Bad Girls, Touching Evil, Coronation Street, London Bridge, Seriously Funny, Thieftakers, Minder, The Bill*.
Radio: *Is He Still Breathing, Life Together, Festen*.

Rob Hastie
William Sharp / Redcoat / Lieutenant

Training: RADA.
Theatre: *The Importance of Being Earnest* (Derby Playhouse), *Nicholas Nickleby* (Chichester), *Great Expectations* (RSC), Edward Bond's *Lear* (Sheffield Crucible), *Forty Years On* (Stephen Joseph Theatre, Scarborough), *The Soldier* (GBS).
Radio: Includes *A Passage to India, Lair of the White Worm, Mr Sex, Black Beauty, King Arthur*.
Winner of BBC Carleton Hobbs Award and member of BBC Radio Drama Company.

Dawn Hope
Phyllis George

Training: Corona Academy London.
Theatre: *Porgy & Bess* (Savoy Theatre), *Bad Girls The Musical* (West Yorkshire Playhouse), *Strange Fruit* (Hong Kong Festival), *Lady Day At Emersons Bar & Grill* (New Players Theatre/National Tour), *Simply Heavenly*

(Trafalgar Studios), *Follow My Leader* (Birmingham Rep/Hampstead Theatre), *Dick Whittington* (Sadlers Wells), *Metropolis Kabaret* (National), *3 Ms Behavin*, (Tricycle Theatre), *Grapevine* (Derby Playhouse), *Ain't Misbehavin'* (Tricycle/Lyric Theatre), *Josephine* (BAC), *Blues in the Night (*Derby Playhouse), *Follow The Star* (Chichester Festival Theatre), *Who's a Lucky Boy* (Manchester Royal Exchange), *West Side Story* (Coventry), *Time* (Dominion Theatre), *Golden Girls* (Ipswich Theatre), *Little Shop of Horrors* (Comedy Theatre), *They're Playing Our Song* (Shaftesbury Theatre), *Chicago* (Cambridge Theatre), *Bubbling Brown Sugar* (Royalty Theatre), *The Black Mikado* (Cambridge Theatre).
Television: Includes *Casualty, Waiting For God, Dempsey & Makepeace, Angels, General Hospital, The Rag Trade, Hey Mr Producer, Heart Surgeon, Comics*.
Film: Includes *Black Joy, Swalk, A Long Way From Home, Midnights Break, Gummed Labels, Richard's Things, Jack of Diamonds*.

Ed Hughes
John Clarkson

Training: Guildhall School of Music and Drama.
Theatre: Includes Candy in *Lovely & Misfit* (Fish Prods/ Trafalgar Studios), Nicholas/Aurelius in *The Canterbury Tales* (RSC/International Tour/West End), Guildenstern in *Hamlet* (Old Vic), Romeo in *Romeo And Juliet* (ETT), Leo Hubbard in *The Little Foxes* (Donmar Warehouse), Fergus in *Finding The Sun* (National), *The Troy Trilogy* (National Theatre Studio), *Candida* (Stephen Joseph Theatre), *Les Liaisons Dangereuses* (National Tour), *Sitting Pretty* (Chelsea Theatre) and *'Tis Pity She's A Whore* (Young Vic).

Television: Includes *Queen of Swords* (Amy International TV) and *David Copperfield* (BBC).
Film: *Incendiary* (2008, Archer Street Films).

Mark Jax
Captain /
Cornwallis /
Falconbridge

Training: RADA.
Theatre: Includes *Mirror For Princes* (Barbican), *Jamaica Inn* (Salisbury Playhouse), *Barbarians* (Salisbury Playhouse), *Laughter on the 23rd Floor* (West End/tour), *Mansfield Park* (Chichester Festival Theatre), *The Norman Conquests* (Salisbury Playhouse), *The Way of the World* (Birmingham Rep), *Macbeth* (Birmingham Rep), *Atheist's Tragedy* (Birmingham Rep), *A Christmas Carol* (Young Vic), *When We Are Married* (West Yorkshire Playhouse), *A Midsummer Night's Dream* (Theatre Royal Plymouth), *Women Beware Women* (Birmingham Rep), *Strange Kind of Animal* (National), *Chorus of Disapproval* (Stephen Joseph Theatre) *Tenant of Wildfell Hall* (Birmingham Rep), *Peter Pan* (Birmingham Rep), *Romeo & Juliet* (Sheffield Crucible), *The Futurists* (National), *Two Planks & a Passion* (Northcott Exeter), *Pravda* (National), *The Government Inspector* (National), *The Devils* (Clwyd Theatr Cymru).
Television: Includes *Marco Polo, Frankenstein, Mary & Jesus, The Two of Us, The Vice, In the Beginning, Casualty, Tales of the Unexpected, Picture of a Woman, Merlin*.
Film: *Stealing Heaven, Living Doll*.

Jessica Lloyd
Young Boy / Anna Maria Falconbridge

Training: Jessica trained at Bristol Old Vic Theatre School.

Theatre: Includes *Under Milk Wood* (Duke's Theatre), *One for the Road* (Coliseum), *The Real Thing* (Royal Theatre), *Abigail's Party* (Duke's Theatre), *Humble Boy* (Library Theatre Manchester), *Season's Greetings* (Theatre By The Lake), *Blithe Spirit* (Theatre By The Lake), *The Tenant of Wildfell Hall* (Theatre By The Lake), *Oedipus Rex* (Nuffield Theatre), *The Memory of Water* (Library Theatre), *Time and the Conways* (Royal Exchange), *Mill on the Floss* (Shared Experience), *Snapshots* (Royal Exchange), *The Ghost Train Tattoo* (Royal Exchange), *Miss Julie* (Nuffield Theatre), *The Bacchae* (Nuffield Theatre), *A Doll's House* (Library Theatre), *War & Peace* (National), *The Importance of Being Earnest* (English Touring Theatre), *Anna Karenina* (Shared Experience), *Lovers, Winners* (Bristol Old Vic).

Television: *Jonathan Creek, Silent Witness, Blooming Marvellous, Poirot, As Time Goes By, Casualty, Head Over Heels*.

Radio: Includes *Hobson's Choice, Under the Spreading Chestnut Tree*.

Film: *Jefferson in Paris*.

Michael Matus
Granville Sharp

Training: RADA.
Theatre: Includes *Mahabharata* (Sadler's Wells), *That Pesky Rat* (Soho Theatre Company), *Canterbury Tales* (RSC West End & Regional Tour), *Comedy of Errors* (Sheffield Theatre), *A Doll's House* (West Yorkshire Playhouse), *Humble Boy* (Northcott Theatre), *The Cherry Orchard* (Oxford Stage Company), *The Venetian Twins* (Watermill Theatre), *The Taming of the Shrew* (Thelma Holt tour), *Hard Times* (Watermill Theatre), *Eating Raoul* (Bridewell Theatre), *The Malcontent* (RSC Swan/Gielgud), *The Island Princess* (RSC Swan/Gielgud), *The Roman Actor* (RSC Swan/Gielgud), *Eastwood Ho!* (RSC Swan/Gielgud), *The Lion, the Witch and The Wardrobe* (RSC Sadlers Wells), *Mill on the Floss* (Shared Experience, Ambassadors/World Tour), *Martin Guerre* (West End), *Sweet Bird of Youth* (Citizens' Theatre), *The Provoked Wife* (Number One Tour), *Marowitz Hamlet* (Citizens' Theatre), *The End of the Affair* (Salisbury Playhouse/Bridewell).

Television: *A Prince Among Men, Then, The Bill, A Perfect World, EastEnders, Dom Joly*.

Film: *A Muppet Christmas Carol*.

Wunmi Mosaku
Sally Peters

Training: Wunmi trained at RADA and recently graduated.
Theatre: *The Great Theatre of the World* (Arcola Theatre).
Television: *Never Better, Weirdos*.
Film: *Women of Troy*.

Ben Okafor
James Somerset

Ben is a prolific singer songwriter, as well as an experienced actor, whose songs and plays frequently address political and human rights issues. As well as composing and performing original music for theatre, Ben has released 10 albums, and will soon embark on his next tour entitled

The Spirit of the Act. This tour will explore the intent and achievement of the 1807 Act to abolish the transatlantic slave trade.

In July this year he starred in the one man-show *Child of Biafra*, based on his own experience as a thirteen-year-old soldier during the Nigeria/Biafra war. Having moved from Nigeria to the UK, Ben began serious acting in 1993 playing various roles including Gower and co-director of music for a touring production of *Pericles* (1996), Jesus in a national tour of *Passion Play* (2000), the lead in *Millennium Man* (2000), composer and performer of music for *African Snow* (2007) and co-writer, composer and performer for *Child of Biafra* (2007). www.benokafor.com

Patrick Robinson
Thomas Peters

Training: LAMDA.

Theatre: Includes *Much Ado About Nothing, King John* (RSC), *Gem of the Ocean* (Tricycle Theatre), *Macbeth* (Out Of Joint), *Festen* (Almeida/Lyric Theatre), *Guantanamo* (Tricycle/Ambassadors), *The Merchant of Venice* (Chichester Festival Theatre), *Mappa Mundi* (National), *Dangerous Corner* (West Yorkshire Playhouse/ Garrick Theatre), *Guess Who's Coming to Dinner* (National Tour), *The Country Wife* (National Tour), *Wuthering Heights* (Chester Gateway), *King Lear, King John, The Plantagenets, Much Ado About Nothing, All God's Children Got Wings, The Great White Hope, They Shoot Horses Don't They?, Macbeth, The Winter's Tale, The Rover, Romeo & Juliet, Twelfth Night* (RSC).
Television: Includes *Tracy Beaker, Shane, Headless, A Many Splintered Thing, Pig Heart Boy, Daylight Robbery, The Man, Harper & Iles, Julius Caesar, Casualty* (series regular).

Film: *Belly of the Beast, The Bee Stung Wasp, Monument, Driven*.
Radio: *The Last Supper, Final Sacrament, Losing Paradise, Cymbeline, One Bright Child, No Man, Blacker than Black*.
Presenting: *Back to the Wild, Windrush Gala Concert, Two Halves Many Colours, Dream Ticket*.

Daniel Williams
Buck Slave / Settler

Training: Daniel trained at the Central School of Speech and Drama where he received the Laurence Olivier Behrens Award.

Theatre: Includes a Shakespeare workshop with English Touring Theatre, *Nakamitsu* (Gate Theatre), *Journeys to Work* (Red Room Theatre Company which was shown in Copenhagen, Denmark), *Unzipped: Unchained* (Soho Theatre in conjunction with Talawa Theatre Company), *Watership Down* (Lyric Hammersmith and UK Tour), *Romeo & Juliet* (Birmingham Rep & UK Tour).
Television: Includes *Tea with Betty* (BBC Afternoon Play), *Mad Dog Days* (ITV Drama), *The Bill*.
Film: Includes *Three for Me* (to be aired later this year), *The Grind* (to be aired later this year).

CREATIVE TEAM

Rupert Goold
Director

Rupert is Artistic Director of Headlong Theatre. Productions for Headlong include *Rough Crossings, Faustus, Restoration* and *Paradise Lost*. From 2002 to 2005 he was Artistic Director of the Royal and Derngate Theatres in Northampton and an Associate Artist at Salisbury Playhouse 1996–97.
Other theatre includes *Macbeth* (Chichester Theatre/Gielgud), *The Glass Menagerie* (Apollo), *The Tempest, Speaking Like Magpies* (RSC), *Scaramouche Jones* (national and international tours), *Gone to LA, Sunday Father* (Hampstead Theatre), *The Colonel Bird* (Gate), *Hamlet, Othello, Waiting for Godot, Insignificance, The Weir, Betrayal, Arcadia, Summer Lightning* (Royal and Derngate Theatres), *The End of the Affair, Dancing at Lughnasa, Habeus Corpus* (Salisbury Playhouse), *Travels with my Aunt* (Salisbury Playhouse/ National Tour), *Broken Glass* (Watford Palace), *Privates on Parade* (New Vic), *The Wind in the Willows* (Birmingham Rep). Opera includes: *Le Comte Ory* (Garsington Opera); *L'Opera Seria, Gli Equivoci, Il Pomo D'Oro* (Batignano).

Laura Hopkins
Designer

Laura designs theatre, opera and experimental performance work. Previous collaborations with Rupert Goold include *Othello*, *Hamlet*, *Le Comte Ory* and *Faustus*, which won the TMA Design Award in 2004.
Recent work includes *Black Watch* (NTS); *The Class Club* (Duckie); *The Three Musketeers* (BOV); *Mercury Fur* (Paines Plough); *The Escapologist* (Suspect Culture); *Macbeth, The Golden Ass* and *The Storm* (all Shakespeare's Globe); *Hotel Methuselah* (Imitating the Dog);

Mister Heracles (WYP, TMA Award for Best Design); *Cosi Fan Tutte* (ENO); *Carnesky's Ghost Train* (a visual theatre ride) and the INS Broadcasting Unit with author Tom McCarthy at the ICA.
Current work includes *Stockholm* by Bryony Lavery (Frantic Assembly), *Kellerman* with Imitating the Dog, *Peer Gynt* with Tim Carroll for the Guthrie theatre and *Office Party Xmas 2007* with Ursula Martinez and Chris Green.

Paul Pyant
Lighting Designer

Paul is a graduate and Associate of RADA.
He has long associations with Glyndebourne Opera, English National Opera, The Royal Opera, Covent Garden, National Theatre, English National Ballet and Northern Ballet Theatre.
Opera work worldwide includes productions in America (Metropolitan Opera, Los Angeles, Houston, Seattle, San Francisco), Australia, New Zealand, France, Holland, Belgium, Israel, Austria, Japan and Italy.
Theatre work includes productions for the Royal Shakespeare Company, the Donmar Warehouse, and productions for London's West End and Broadway in New York.
Work in ballet has included productions for the Royal New Zealand Ballet, the Norwegian National Ballet, Boston Ballet, Milwaukee Ballet, Atlanta Ballet, Colorado Ballet and the Asami Maki Ballet in Tokyo.
Over the last year productions have included: *A Midsummer Night's Dream* (dir. Peter Hall) and *Die Fledermaus* (dir. Stephen Lawless) at Glyndebourne Festival Opera, *The Gondoliers* (Martin Duncan) for English National Opera, *Anna Karenina* (dir. Michael Barker-Graven) at the Gate Theatre Dublin, *Turn of the Screw* (dir. Tim Carroll) Opera de Oviedo, Spain, *The Glass Menagerie* (dir. Rupert Goold), Apollo Theatre, London, *Stiffelio* (dir. Elijah

Moshinsky) Royal Opera, Covent Garden London and *The Lord of the Rings* (dir. Matthew Warchus) at the Theatre Royal Drury Lane.

A more detailed biography can be viewed at www.theatricaldesigners.co.uk.

Adam Cork
Composer & Sound Designer

Adam Cork read music at Cambridge University, studying composition with Robin Holloway.

Theatre: Scores and sound designs for *Frost/Nixon* (Donmar/Gielgud/ Broadway), *Suddenly Last Summer* (Albery), *Don Carlos* (Gielgud), *The Glass Menagerie* (Apollo), *Speaking Like Magpies* (RSC Swan), *The Tempest* (RSC RST/Michigan/Novello), *Caligula, The Wild Duck, Don Juan in Soho, John Gabriel Borkman* (Donmar), *The Late Henry Moss, Tom & Viv* (Almeida), *On the Third Day* (New Ambassadors, subject of Channel 4 documentary 'The Play's the Thing'), *Underneath the Lintel* (Duchess), *On The Ceiling* (Garrick), *Scaramouche Jones* (Riverside Studios/World Tour), *Troilus and Cressida* (Old Vic), *Faustus* (Headlong/ Hampstead Theatre), *Paradise Lost* (Oxford Stage Company/Headlong), *Nine Parts of Desire* (Wilma Theatre Philadelphia), *Lear, The Cherry Orchard* (Sheffield Crucible), *Romeo and Juliet* (Manchester Royal Exchange), *The Government Inspector* (Chichester Festival), *Macbeth* (Chichester Minerva), *My Uncle Arly* (Royal Opera House Linbury), *The Field* (Tricycle), *Alice's Adventures in Wonderland* (Bristol Old Vic, received 2005 TMA Award Best Show for Young People). Adam was nominated for the 2005 Olivier Award for Best Sound Design for *Suddenly Last Summer* (Albery). He also received a 2007 'Outstanding Music for a Play' Drama Desk Award nomination, for the Broadway production of *Frost/Nixon*.

Film/TV: Includes *Frances Tuesday* (ITV1), *Re-ignited, Imprints* (both Channel 4), *Bust* (Film Council), *The Three Rules of Infidelity* (Illyria films), *Sexdrive* (Vancouver Film Festival), *Tripletake* (JJC Films).

Radio: Includes *Losing Rosalind, The Luneberg Variation* (both BBC Radio 4), *The Colonel-Bird* (BBC World Service), *Don Carlos* (BBC Radio 3).

Lorna Heavey
Video & Projection Designer

Video design credits include *Macbeth* (West End & Minerva, Chichester), *I Am Shakespeare,* (Minerva, Chichester), *The Caucasian Chalk Circle* (National Theatre), *The Tempest* (RSC, West End), *Speaking Like Magpies* (RSC, Swan), *Phaedra* (Donmar), *Vanishing Point, Genoa 01* (Complicite, Royal Court), *Faustus, Paradise Lost* (Headlong), *Cooped* (Purcell Rooms & international tour), *Tall Phoenix* (Belgrade), *Betrayal* (Northampton), *Cleansed* (Arcola), *I Am Thicker Than Water* (This Way Up Tour), *The Waves* (BAC), *Mahabharata* (Sadler's Wells), *Dido And Aeneas* (Opera North), *Very Opera* (Cologne). Set design includes *Hamlet Machine* (KunstHalle Berlin & BAC), *Trajectory* (European tour), *Titus Andronicus* (BAC), *A Stitch In Time, Beautiful Beginnings* (Theatre 503).

Writing & directing credits include *A Stitch In Time, Beautiful Beginnings, Several Words* (Split & Hanover Film Festival), *Timed Existence* (Edinburgh Film Festival), *The Global Conditioned, Duet for One Voice* (Film Festival, Berlin), *Interior/Exterior* (Roppongi Tokyo).

Art Exhibitions include shows at ICA, RIBA, Dada Dandies Berlin, Poznan Poland, Budapest Academy.

Founder and artistic director of Headfirst Foundation, a cross platform artists' collective. Trained in Fine Art at Düsseldorf Art Academy (nam June Paik & nan Hoover), Kingston University, Chelsea School of Art.

Elected Fellow of The Royal Society of Arts in 2004.

Liz Ranken
Movement Director

Performer: Founder member DV8, Gloria Music Theatre, Cat A (touring prisons and theatres), and the Grassmarket project. Liz was artist in residence at CCA Glasgow (choreographer and performer). Her own work includes *Summat A do wi weddins* which won the Place Portfolio award and *Funk off Green* which won the Capital Award Edinburgh. Liz has appeared in the feature films *Edward II* directed by Derek Jarman and *3 Steps to Heaven* directed by Connie Giannaris.

Movement Director: Liz is Associate Movement Director for the RST and Shared Experience. Her work includes *The History Cycle* (RSC), *Mill on the Floss*, *Anna Karenina*, *Jane Eyre* (Shared Experience). Liz has also worked extensively with Dominic Cooke, both at the RSC and the Royal Court. Credits include *Fire Face*, *The Winter's Tale*, *Pericles* and *Arabian Nights*.

Liz won the Time Out award for bringing theatre alive with movement. She also paints professionally.

Headlong

Headlong Theatre is dedicated to new ways of making theatre. By exploring revolutionary writers and practitioners of the past and commissioning new work from artists from a wide variety of backgrounds we aim constantly to push the imaginative boundaries of the stage. Headlong makes exhilarating, provocative and spectacular new work to take around the country and around the world.

For more information or to join our mailing list, please go to: www.headlongtheatre.co.uk

Coming soon from Headlong:

Marlowe's *Faustus* in a new version by Rupert Goold and Ben Power

The Last Days of Judas Iscariot by Stephen Adly Guirgis

'Headlong's first season is a mouthwatering array of major works' (*Telegraph*)

'One of our most exciting and flamboyant directors' (*Time Out* on Rupert Goold)

Artistic Director **Rupert Goold**
Executive Producer **Henny Finch**
Finance Manager **Julie Renwick**
Literary Associate **Ben Power**
Assistant Producer **Jenni Kershaw**

ᴛʜᴇREP
Birmingham Repertory Theatre

Birmingham Repertory Theatre is one of Britain's leading national producing theatre companies. From its base in Birmingham, The REP produces over twenty new productions each year.

Having recently taken over as Artistic Director, Rachel Kavanaugh has just announced her second season of work, for Autumn 2007. Highlights of the season include this production of *Rough Crossings*, a fresh new revival of *Brief Encounter* co-produced with Kneehigh, *She Stoops to Conquer*, the UK premiere of Bryony Lavery's *Last Easter* and the first full-scale theatre production of George Stiles and Anthony Drewe's musical version of *Peter Pan*.

The commissioning and production of new work lies at the core of The REP's programme giving world premieres of new plays from a new generation of British playwrights. The REP's productions regularly transfer to London and tour nationally and internationally. Recent transfers and tours have included *Glorious!*, *The Birthday Party*, *Of Mice And Men*, *A Doll's House*, *The Crucible*, *Celestina*, *Hamlet*, *The Old Masters*, *The Snowman*, and *The Ramayana*.

Artistic Director **Rachel Kavanaugh**
Executive Director **Stuart Rogers**
Associate Director (Literary) **Ben Payne**

Book online at www.birmingham-rep.co.uk
Birmingham Repertory Theatre is a registered charity, number 223660

EVERYMAN LIVERPOOL PLAYHOUSE

As Liverpool prepares to take on the mantle of European Capital of Culture in 2008, the Everyman and Playhouse are experiencing a dramatic upsurge in creative activity; producing critically acclaimed in house work as well as welcoming some of the best touring work from around the UK and Europe.

But there is more to these theatres than simply the work on our stages. We have a busy Literary Department, working to nurture the next generation of Liverpool playwrights. A wide-ranging Community Department takes our work to all corners of the city and surrounding areas, and works in partnership with schools, colleges, youth and community groups to open up the theatre to all.

Our aim is for these theatres to be an engine for creative excellence, artistic adventure, and audience involvement; firmly rooted in our community, yet both national and international in scope and ambition.

Artistic Director **Gemma Bodinetz**
Executive Director **Deborah Aydon**

www.everymanplayhouse.com

The Lyric Hammersmith has a national reputation for creating work that takes theatre in new and bold directions.

Over the past ten years we have worked with some of theatre's most groundbreaking artists including Improbable Theatre, Kneehigh, Frantic Assembly, Iceland's Vesturport and Headlong. Collaboration is central to everything we do, as we invite the most exciting and audacious artists to work together to tell stories that resonate with a modern audience.

Integral to our work on stage is our commitment to providing opportunities for young people to achieve their potential. Our Creative Learning Department delivers a comprehensive programme of activities, linked to our productions, helping schools to deliver the National Curriculum. We also run a wide range of activities outside school hours for young West Londoners from all backgrounds, helping them to learn new skills, make new friends, gain qualifications and work experience.

At the heart of the Lyric's work is a focus on the creative development of the individual, from artists to audiences, all in the passionate belief that theatre can change people's lives.

Artistic Director **David Farr**
Executive Director **Jessica Hepburn**

www.lyric.co.uk

^{WY}PLAY HOUSE

West Yorkshire Playhouse has a reputation both nationally and internationally as one of Britain's most exciting and active producing theatres. The Playhouse provides both a thriving focal point for the communities of West Yorkshire and theatre of the highest standard for audiences throughout the region and beyond.

Programming regularly includes collaborations with other major regional producing theatres and companies including: Kneehigh Theatre, Birmingham Repertory Theatre Company, Liverpool Everyman and Playhouse, Northern Broadsides, Polka and Lyric Hammersmith.

Recent West End transfers have included: *Ying Tong* (2004) to the New Ambassadors, *The Postman Always Rings Twice* (2005) to the Playhouse Theatre, the Olivier award-winning *The 39 Steps* (2005) which is currently playing at the Criterion Theatre, *The Hound of the Baskervilles* (2007) at the Duchess Theatre and, following its World Premiere at the Playhouse in 2006, *Bad Girls – The Musical* which will be playing at the Garrick Theatre this autumn.

Artistic Director & Chief Executive **Ian Brown**
Director of Operations **Helen Child**
Producer **Henrietta Duckworth**
Finance Director **Caroline Harrison**
Executive Director **Lesley Jackson**
Director of Communications **Su Matthewman**
Director of Arts Development **Sam Perkins**

www.wyp.org.uk

ROUGH CROSSINGS

ROUGH CROSSINGS

by Simon Schama

Adapted for the stage
by Caryl Phillips

OBERON BOOKS
LONDON

First published in this adaptation in 2007 by Oberon Books Ltd
521 Caledonian Road, London N7 9RH
Tel: 020 7607 3637 / Fax: 020 7607 3629
email: info@oberonbooks.com
www.oberonbooks.com

Rough Crossings adaptation © copyright Caryl Phillips 2007

based on *Rough Crossings* © copyright Simon Schama 2005

Caryl Phillips is hereby identified as author of this adaptation in
accordance with section 77 of the Copyright, Designs and Patents
Act 1988. The author has asserted his moral rights.

All rights whatsoever in this adaptation are strictly reserved
and application for performance etc. should be made before
commencement of rehearsal to Judy Daish Associates Limited,
2 St Charles Place, London W10 6EG. No performance may
be given unless a licence has been obtained, and no alterations
may be made in the title or the text of the adaptation without the
author's prior written consent.

This book is sold subject to the condition that it shall not by way
of trade or otherwise be circulated without the publisher's consent
in any form of binding or cover, stored in a retrieval system or
circulated electronically other than that in which it is published
and without a similar condition including this condition being
imposed on any subsequent purchaser.

A catalogue record for this book is available from the British
Library.

Cover design by Eureka! Design.

ISBN: 1 84002 804 1 / 978-1-84002-804-1

Printed in Great Britain by Antony Rowe Ltd, Chippenham.

For James Walvin

Characters

in order of appearance

SHIP'S BOY

CAPTAIN

JOHNSON

THOMAS PETERS

BUCK SLAVE

ELIZA SHARP

WILLIAM SHARP

GRANVILLE SHARP

THOMAS CLARKSON

JOHN CLARKSON

DAVID GEORGE

PHYLLIS GEORGE

SALLY PETERS

ISAAC

REDCOAT

AUCTIONEER

BIDDER

JAMES SOMERSET

SERGEANT DAVY

LORD CHIEF JUSTICE MANSFIELD

ASSOCIATE JUSTICES

GENERAL LORD CHARLES CORNWALLIS

LIEUTENANT

OFFICER

AMERICAN OFFICER

KING JIMMY

INDENTURED MAN

ALEXANDER FALCONBRIDGE

ANNA MARIA FALCONBRIDGE

MR GREEN

MR WILSON

ISAAC'S FATHER

JAILER

and

Slaves, Sailors, Soldiers, Drummers, Attendants, Slave Owners, Slave Traders, Servants, Sierra Leonean Settlers, Nova Scotian Settlers.

Act One

We hear the sound of the loud engine of the sea, the creaking of wood, and the clanging of metal chains. Lights slowly up. An occasional voice is raised in misery. A SHIP'S BOY, in white shirt, knee breeches and bare feet, bursts onto the deck of the ship from below. He looks anxiously around.

SHIP'S BOY: Sir? (*Pause. To himself.*) Oh bloody hell. (*Shouts.*) Sir?

(*Out of the gloom steps the CAPTAIN. He is formally dressed, in a naval jacket. He presses a handkerchief to his nose and mouth.*)

CAPTAIN: I can hear you, my lad.

SHIP'S BOY: I'm sorry, sir. I didn't see you over there.

CAPTAIN: If you desire to live long enough to take a young girl for a wife, you had better learn to stand upwind on a slaving ship and away from disease.

SHIP'S BOY: Yes sir.

CAPTAIN: Do you have a sweetheart waiting for you back in London?

SHIP'S BOY: London, sir?

CAPTAIN: You *are* a Londoner, aren't you?

SHIP'S BOY: Yes sir. Bow bells, sir.

CAPTAIN: And do you have a sweetheart?

SHIP'S BOY: A sweetheart, sir?

CAPTAIN: A creature who you love and cherish, and who you might one day be joined together with in holy matrimony.

SHIP'S BOY: No, sir. Sorry, sir.

(*Sound of shouting and heavy feet coming closer.*)

CAPTAIN: No need to apologize. But don't end up like me, with no wife, and no children, and only a mistress called the ocean for company. (*Pause.*) And why are we here on the ocean, my lad?

SHIP'S BOY: Don't know, sir.

CAPTAIN: Profit, my lad. Not duty, or honour. Profit! (*Pause.*) You want to say something, lad?

SHIP'S BOY: Please sir, it's the prime niggers. They're bringing them up now, but there's some sickness.

CAPTAIN: And the buck nigger?

SHIP'S BOY: Not ailing sir, but not broken either. He has the look in his eye, sir.

(*JOHNSON, an older sailor in his thirties, and of a low rank, emerges on deck from below. He sees the SHIP'S BOY.*)

JOHNSON: (*To SHIP'S BOY.*) You little arse-rag, didn't you hear me calling you? (*He then sees the CAPTAIN.*) Sorry sir, didn't see you standing there. I was looking for laddie boy here. Prime niggers coming up for inspection and dancing, but we've some spoilt cargo to unload.

CAPTAIN: It's all insured, Mr Johnson. Apparently, we can't show mercy and risk infecting the whole cargo.

JOHNSON: 'Apparently', sir?

CAPTAIN: Well is mercy permissible?

JOHNSON: Sorry, sir. Not following you that well.

CAPTAIN: Fatigue, Mr Johnson. This voyage. All voyages. For heaven's sake, Mr Johnson. You know what to do.

JOHNSON: (*Shouts.*) Bring 'em up.

(*We hear the sound of a drum being beaten and then see a white DRUMMER BOY emerge from below. Behind him are six male SLAVES all chained together, attired only in loincloths. Their bodies are scarred and pockmarked, their hair bushy and unkempt, and they are escorted by four WHITE SAILORS with muskets who keep a close watch and prod them when necessary. The SLAVES line up and JOHNSON takes a piece of metal and*) *begins to force open their mouths and inspect their teeth and gums. One SLAVE among them, THOMAS PETERS, looks particularly weak. He is being examined.*)

This one's ailing, sir.

CAPTAIN: The man's frightened, Mr Johnson.

JOHNSON: Don't like to think of them as men, sir.

CAPTAIN: Surely fear is a human disease? Curable, even.

(*JOHNSON continues to inspect the SLAVES. The final and strongest-looking SLAVE is defiant as his mouth is forced open.*)

JOHNSON: Captain, the buck nigger's real trouble.

CAPTAIN: Then you must tame him, Mr Johnson.

(*JOHNSON puts away his piece of metal. He unfurls a whip and begins to thrash at them.*)

JOHNSON: Dance, you bastards. Dance!

(*Some among the SLAVES clearly have little energy to move and they are ailing badly. The 'BUCK' SLAVE refuses to dance.*)

CAPTAIN: (*To SHIP'S BOY.*) The rum.

(*The CAPTAIN has spoken into his handkerchief so the SHIP'S BOY is not entirely sure of what the CAPTAIN has said.*)

SHIP'S BOY: Sir?

CAPTAIN: (*Takes away the handkerchief.*) The rum, boy. Now! (*The SHIP'S BOY scampers away. To the DRUMMER BOY.*) Keep a steady beat, man. This is not some jungle ceremony. (*JOHNSON continues to thrash the slaves who have difficulty dancing.*) Tell me, Mr Johnson. From where in England do you originate?

JOHNSON: Norfolk, sir. Born and bred.

CAPTAIN: I thought so. Your accent. (*Somewhat reflectively.*) Tess was her name. A farmer's daughter from Norfolk. Tess Warner.

JOHNSON: Sir?

(*The SHIP'S BOY reappears with a flask of rum which he hands to the CAPTAIN. The CAPTAIN grabs it and takes a deep drink.*)

CAPTAIN: (*Laughs.*) This civilizing mission can be damned exhausting work.

JOHNSON: It's God's work, sir. The price of being an Englishman.

CAPTAIN: (*To SHIP'S BOY.*) You hear that boy? Are you ready to pay the price and exchange London for the ocean wide, the ocean blue?

SHIP'S BOY: I was pressed into service, sir.

CAPTAIN: (*Laughs. To JOHNSON.*) The young boy claims to have been pressed against his will. Like a delicate flower in a book. (*Offers a toast.*) To England.

JOHNSON: To England!

CAPTAIN: (*Points at the strongest-looking SLAVE.*) He's still not dancing, Mr Johnson.

JOHNSON: Can't break the buck, sir.

BUCK SLAVE: (*The SLAVES all speak in a West African language.*) I will kill you, white man. All of you.

CAPTAIN: What did he say?

JOHNSON: (*Whips him.*) Quiet!

BUCK SLAVE: (*To his fellow SLAVES.*) Once we cross this mighty river we shall be free of these men. Look at them, they are no match for us. Even in this condition we frighten them.

JOHNSON: Time to cut our losses, sir.

SLAVE 2: But we must fight them now. We can take their guns.

SLAVE 3: He is right. They will kill more of us if we do not act.

BUCK SLAVE: No. We must act only when we are sure of victory.

SLAVE 2: And meanwhile we live as cowards? My death must mean something.

BUCK SLAVE: My life must mean something!

SLAVE 2: But you are not in control of your life! Our death must mean something or this pain and suffering has been for nothing.

JOHNSON: (*Points to 'THOMAS PETERS'.*) This one is too weak. (*To the SAILORS with muskets.*) Unchain him.

SLAVE / 'THOMAS PETERS': They are going to put me overboard.

JOHNSON: Shut it! (*Lashes 'THOMAS PETERS'.*) And him. (*Points to SLAVE 3. SLAVE 3 is also unchained.*)

SLAVE / 'THOMAS PETERS': They are going to kill us. We must do something!

SLAVE 3: (*To the 'BUCK SLAVE'.*) And are you now happy? You are to live and we two are to die!

(*JOHNSON takes out a stick and begins to push and prod the two unchained SLAVES to the edge of the ship.*)

SLAVE 2: Let them hear our voices.

(*The SLAVES begin to chant defiantly, all except the 'BUCK SLAVE'.*)

SLAVE / 'THOMAS PETERS': (*To the other SLAVES.*) Are we to die like this? Without a fight?

SLAVE 3: (*To SLAVE / 'THOMAS PETERS'.*) Hold up your head and die like a man.

SHIP'S BOY: (*To CAPTAIN.*) What are they saying, sir?

CAPTAIN: That's how the blacks say goodbye to their kin.

JOHNSON: (*Points to SLAVE 3.*) Over the side with him.

(*Two SAILORS grab SLAVE 3 and heave him over the side of the ship. We hear him scream and then hit the water. The SLAVES continue to chant defiantly; with the exception of the 'BUCK SLAVE'.*)

SHIP'S BOY: (*To CAPTAIN.*) Please sir, I want to go home.

(*The CAPTAIN takes a swig of rum and then tosses the flask into the sea.*)

JOHNSON: The other nigger.

(*As the SAILORS grab SLAVE / 'THOMAS PETERS', the 'BUCK SLAVE' rushes at the SAILORS and strikes out at them. The 'BUCK' struggles with the SAILORS.*)

(*To the other SAILORS.*) Don't shoot him! Captain's profit's in that nigger.

(*The struggle continues, but the 'BUCK SLAVE' is becoming increasingly dominant and it looks like the other SLAVES might join in.*)

CAPTAIN: Mr Johnson, dispatch him.

JOHNSON: But Captain…

CAPTAIN: That's an order, Mr Johnson. Quell the rebellion.

(*JOHNSON grabs a musket and fires once into the heart of the 'BUCK SLAVE' who falls down dead. The CAPTAIN points to SLAVE / 'THOMAS PETERS'.*)

Chain that man, then put the dead man overboard.

JOHNSON: He was your most valuable cargo, sir.

CAPTAIN: (*Laughs.*) I am the most valuable cargo on this ship, Mr Johnson.

JOHNSON: Yes, sir. (*Points to SLAVE / 'THOMAS PETERS'.*) This one might not make it all the way to America.

CAPTAIN: (*Laughs.*) Shall we pray for him?

(*JOHNSON begins to chain the four remaining SLAVES to each other. The SLAVES begin again to chant. SLAVE / 'THOMAS PETERS' seems too weak to chant.*)

SLAVE 2: Let them hear our voices. If we are brought out on deck again, then we must act together.

(*The SHIP'S BOY begins to back away. The CAPTAIN sees him.*)

CAPTAIN: Stand still! Are you afraid?

SHIP'S BOY: No, sir. I mean, yes sir.

JOHNSON: No room for fear in this new world. It's them or us, my boy. You had better decide whose side you're on.

(*The CAPTAIN begins to sing a hymn, as though trying to drown
out the sound of the SLAVES and their chanting. JOHNSON joins
him, as do the SAILORS with muskets. Eventually they drown out
the chanting of the African SLAVES, who stop singing. They look
at the WHITE MEN singing and realize that the WHITE MEN have
won this particular skirmish. But there is a look of defiance on
their faces. The WHITE MEN continue to sing their hymn.*)

SCENE TWO

*We hear the strains of Handel emerging from the darkness. The
music begins to rise to a crescendo and then it finishes. There is light
applause.*

*Lights. We see the SHARP FAMILY – ELIZA at the harpsichord, WILLIAM
at the organ, and GRANVILLE on double flute. They are taking a bow as
they gently float down the River Thames on their barge. This evening's
guests are THOMAS CLARKSON, a bluff man in his forties, and his
younger brother, JOHN CLARKSON, who has on his naval uniform.*

THOMAS CLARKSON: Excellent, excellent. But is that all? My
brother and I demand more from the musical Sharp family.

ELIZA SHARP: (*Leaving her harpsichord.*) You 'demand' more,
Mr Clarkson?

THOMAS CLARKSON: Well, it is a pity that such great pleasure
should be so brief.

WILLIAM SHARP: Indeed, it is the tragedy of man that we
should be rewarded with such brief moments of pleasure.

THOMAS CLARKSON: Do you speak now as a medical man?

GRANVILLE SHARP: My brother is both a doctor and a
musician. He combines a disciplined scientific mind, with a
more reflective muse.

THOMAS CLARKSON: But in this particular case, which does
triumph?

ELIZA SHARP: My brother's impure mind when he has
forgotten the presence of a lady, albeit his younger sister.
(*To WILLIAM SHARP.*) Surely the king's surgeon has no need
to attempt such base witticisms.

WILLIAM SHARP: My dear Eliza, I meant to cause no offence to your ears.

ELIZA SHARP: My ears? It is your eyes that concern me, dear Doctor Sharp. You do not see me, which is why you feel free to speak in this manner.

THOMAS CLARKSON: Now, now. I won't have squabbling between brother and sister. Especially when I'm here on a matter of such urgency.

WILLIAM SHARP: Do you consider recruiting a simple doctor to your abolitionist cause a matter of great urgency?

THOMAS CLARKSON: But you're the king's doctor, Mr Sharp. You're a man of considerable influence. Have you no interest in abolishing the evil of slavery?

ELIZA SHARP: (*Laughs.*) In our world we do not view everything through the window of slavery.

THOMAS CLARKSON: I beg your pardon?

ELIZA SHARP: I am merely trying to be helpful, Mr Clarkson. Have you no other type of conversation?

THOMAS CLARKSON: Excuse me, young lady, but I am addressing your brother.

WILLIAM SHARP: I am sure there are others more qualified than I who are able to speak to the condition of the blacks in our kingdom and abroad. However, my principal worry is that we may soon find ourselves undone by these American colonial rebels. Surely, at a time such as this, 'blacky' is an exotic concern with which to occupy an educated English mind.

THOMAS CLARKSON: An exotic concern? Is there anything more important than a man's liberty? A man must be free to govern himself, and to determine how, where, and for whom, he chooses to labour.

ELIZA SHARP: (*To JOHN CLARKSON.*) And what say you on this matter, Lieutenant Clarkson? You appear to have misplaced your tongue.

THOMAS CLARKSON: My brother John is of a shy and modest disposition, unlike yourself, young lady.

ELIZA SHARP: Presumably you prefer your female company to be silent and compliant. Much like your negroes.

THOMAS CLARKSON: I have no negroes!

ELIZA SHARP: But I understand you continually speak on their behalf as though they were bereft of tongues.

WILLIAM SHARP: Now, now, Eliza, you know full well that Mr Thomas Clarkson is one of the cleverest men of this, or any other, age.

THOMAS CLARKSON: (*To ELIZA SHARP.*) Negroes are not able to articulate the full extent of their misery.

ELIZA SHARP: And you, of course, are profoundly aware of the full extent of their misery? (*To JOHN CLARKSON.*) And you, sir. Have you ever spoken with a negro?

JOHN CLARKSON: Not directly, although I have served in His Majesty's Navy in the West Indies. I have laid eyes upon many negroes.

ELIZA SHARP: So, unlike your brother, *you* have some idea of the extent of these creatures' misery. Perhaps you have been responsible for their unhappiness?

THOMAS CLARKSON: Miss Sharp, my brother John is a naval man who has avoided the vast profits and moral degradation of debasing his skills in the slaving business. There have been many offers.

ELIZA SHARP: Have there indeed? I am sure.

WILLIAM SHARP: (*Plays a few chords on the organ.*) Shall we return to our recital?

THOMAS CLARKSON: A splendid idea.

ELIZA SHARP: But why conclude our conversation?

THOMAS CLARKSON: Because you, Miss Sharp, seem determined to mock our ideals. In the face of your provocation we are all struggling to maintain some vestige of decorum.

ELIZA SHARP: How very noble of you, Mr Clarkson. Decorum and your precious ideals.

THOMAS CLARKSON: Yes, they *are* precious ideals! (*To WILLIAM.*) Pray continue the concert, William.

ELIZA SHARP: Yet your ideals have not hindered your own profits.

THOMAS CLARKSON: Ideals are not incompatible with profit. And my profits are not made from trading in black carcasses.

ELIZA SHARP: Well, I for one think there are far too many of these people in our world. And they do seem determined to congregate on the lowest rungs of society.

GRANVILLE SHARP: But my dear sister, their low status is hardly their own fault.

ELIZA SHARP: Oh Granville, please. With the application of hard work, and a little good fortune, any man can rise. These men of intelligence, who specialize in negro charity, are we to trust their motives?

THOMAS CLARKSON: Madam, I am motivated by my conscience.

ELIZA SHARP: But why do you sacrifice so much for these African creatures?

THOMAS CLARKSON: My conscience alone is my guide! I will not rest until it is clearly written in the laws of our land that these people are not property to be used, abused, and discarded at will.

ELIZA SHARP: (*Laughs.*) And you believe that the laws of England can be changed to deliberately end the most profitable business ever known to man?

THOMAS CLARKSON: Madam, I believe that an appeal to the conscience of ordinary English people will ensure that Parliament will eventually have no choice but to recognize the truth concerning this evil trade.

JOHN CLARKSON: Perhaps we need to hear directly from the negroes themselves.

ELIZA SHARP: Hurrah, Mr Clarkson. You have discovered your tongue.

JOHN CLARKSON: I assure you it was not lost. I was merely meditating upon these issues. Perhaps an appeal from black and white together might sway the general and affect Parliament.

THOMAS CLARKSON: But there are no blacks who are qualified to speak.

GRANVILLE SHARP: What is the qualification?

THOMAS CLARKSON: I tell you, there are none who are able.

GRANVILLE SHARP: Can this be true?

WILLIAM SHARP: I am sorry, Mr Clarkson, but I still find 'blacky' an exotic and somewhat irrelevant concern. Let him not affect our mood in this manner.

THOMAS CLARKSON: It is our duty to help these people by bringing their cases into our law courts.

GRANVILLE SHARP: I am ignorant of many of the details of your campaigning. Can any of these cases be won?

THOMAS CLARKSON: Sadly, English justice would appear to be colour-conscious.

GRANVILLE SHARP: But would a legal victory guarantee their freedom?

ELIZA SHARP: Oh, Granville, one moment it is accounting. The next translation. Now it is this amateur interest in the law. You appear to be a gawkish bird in flight and my dearest wish is that you should land safely and settle on one career, be it law or something else.

THOMAS CLARKSON: Madam, the law is the basis of our civilization.

ELIZA SHARP: And should you achieve some sort of legal victory do you wish these people to be your neighbours?

Like the good Dr Johnson, are you willing to take them into your families? (*Pause.*) Well?

THOMAS CLARKSON: Are you perhaps thinking of taking a negro for a husband, Miss Sharp?

ELIZA SHARP: And by doing so bind inferior bondsman to inferior bondswoman and thereafter plead for your tolerance? I think not, Mr Clarkson. I grudgingly applaud your ideals, but your sense of humour is a trifle offensive.

JOHN CLARKSON: I am sure that my brother intends to cause no offence, Miss Sharp. He possesses the same admirable determination that you exhibit.

ELIZA SHARP: Is that so? (*Points.*) We are once again approaching my brother's paymaster. Enough of Mr Clarkson's ideals. An air for the king.

WILLIAM SHARP: (*Begins to play the organ.*) A melody with which we are all familiar.

(*GRANVILLE SHARP joins his brother WILLIAM. ELIZA takes up her place at the harpsichord and begins to play.*)

SCENE THREE

We see DAVID GEORGE, a dignified black man in his forties, who holds a Bible in one hand. He is preaching in a clear, firm voice. The sound of gunfire punctuates what he says. He often looks up in the direction of the battle. We realize that we are in some kind of rudimentary plantation hut. PHYLLIS GEORGE, a black woman in her thirties, is listening to her husband, along with other SLAVES. We recognize THOMAS PETERS from Scene One. He stands by the door, aside from the others, with his wife, SALLY PETERS.

DAVID GEORGE: Listen to the noise of the battle as it approaches. Our American masters have fled, but they still want us to remain here as their slaves. However, the British need our help and in return they offer us freedom. By understanding and accepting the ways of our Lord Jesus Christ, I have found the strength to endure all that life has placed in front of me as an obstacle to my happiness.

Patience is a virtue, but there comes a time to act. My God knows this. It is all written in this book. We cannot be patient forever.

THOMAS PETERS: I am leaving. I cannot listen to this man.

SALLY PETERS: Leaving to go where? Thomas, we all have to stay together.

THOMAS PETERS: Because this man can read the white man's words, does this make him better than everybody else?

SALLY PETERS: He is trying to help.

THOMAS PETERS: The man was born in this country. Look at him! He is almost a white man.

DAVID GEORGE: This is an undignified and barbarous captivity in the eyes of our Lord and saviour, and now is the time to seize our chance and liberate ourselves.

THOMAS PETERS: (*Points.*) Do you truly wish to follow this preacher man?

SALLY PETERS: He is right. (*Pause.*) The people respect you, Thomas, but you have not proposed a plan. We must make a choice. We either stay on this plantation as slaves or we go to the British.

THOMAS PETERS: So you are with him?

SALLY PETERS: I am with you, my husband. And the child in my belly.

DAVID GEORGE: It is time! Are there any of you who are content to be slaves in this American world?

THOMAS PETERS: David George! I am not a slave.

DAVID GEORGE: But Thomas, you are the property of a white man as we all are.

THOMAS PETERS: He can never own what is in my heart or in my mind. I am a slave to no man.

DAVID GEORGE: (*Points to the Bible.*) The words of this good book state clearly that all men are free. We are all equal in the eyes of the Lord.

(*We hear loud gunfire and it causes panic in the room.*)

THOMAS PETERS: (*Calmly.*) There is no reason to be alarmed. The British gunfire is still distant.

DAVID GEORGE: But the battle comes towards us and we must choose.

THOMAS PETERS: (*Laughs.*) We must choose between white American men who claim to own us, or white British men who do not wish to lose their colony.

DAVID GEORGE: Once the British have put down this uprising, they have promised to guarantee our freedom.

THOMAS PETERS: They say this only because they are desperate for us to fight their war for them.

DAVID GEORGE: With them.

THOMAS PETERS: For them, with them, it matters little how you phrase it. But why should we risk our lives for these British? Why should we trust them?

DAVID GEORGE: Because they have made a promise.

THOMAS PETERS: Will the child in my wife's belly truly be free if we fight with these British? (*Points.*) Can *you* guarantee that to me?

PHYLLIS GEORGE: Thomas, my husband is saying that if we fight with the British then we are fighting for our freedom. If this American rebellion succeeds then we will be slaves forever.

THOMAS PETERS: We are not slaves!

DAVID GEORGE: Then why do we stay here in these conditions? Why do we not just walk away?

ISAAC: (*A man in his thirties.*) Because they will kill us, we know this. But Thomas Peters is asking, are the British any better than the Americans?

THOMAS PETERS: Exactly! Thank you, Isaac. (*To DAVID GEORGE.*) What is it about these British that you love?

(*There is the sound of more gunfire in the distance.*)

DAVID GEORGE: Love? I love only my God. And my wife, Phyllis.

PHYLLIS GEORGE: Thomas, why are you so angry? Look at us. We are all the same. (*THOMAS PETERS laughs.*) What does your laughter mean?

ISAAC: Let us not fight amongst each other.

DAVID GEORGE: I shall lead the men to enlist with the redcoats. It is to their side that we must march.

THOMAS PETERS: Is this the feeling of every man here? (*Nobody says anything.*) Are there not some among you who feel ashamed to put on the white man's uniform and do his killing for him?

VOICE 1: Thomas, if we remain here we shall die.

VOICE 2: (*To THOMAS PETERS.*) David George is right. The man who owns us will always think he owns us. We must leave.

(*Everybody begins to gather around DAVID GEORGE.*)

DAVID GEORGE: Come with us, Thomas. If you stay behind the Americans will assume you had knowledge of our escape and they may well punish you with death.

(*We hear the sound of drumbeats, which steadily become louder.*)

Thomas, I give you one last chance to join with us.

THOMAS PETERS: Are you now my leader? (*To ISAAC.*) Isaac?

ISAAC: I will stay.

THOMAS PETERS: No, Isaac, go. But keep your ears and your eyes open.

DAVID GEORGE: (*To those assembled.*) Come we must go to the British.

SALLY PETERS: Thomas, please. Are we to stay here alone?

(*A clearly distraught SALLY stands with THOMAS PETERS, and they watch DAVID GEORGE lead the MEN and WOMEN towards the BRITISH. A white DRUMMER, together with a British REDCOAT, marches on to the stage. The REDCOAT begins to shout.*)

41

REDCOAT: Line up, line up! Come on, move. (*The black SLAVES begin to form a line and stand in front of the REDCOAT.*) You have willingly fled your plantation in order that you might fight for King George III of England, who entrusts me with the task of first thanking you, and then insisting that I turn you scruffy rabble into soldiers fit to represent His Majesty. Now then, off with your rags. (*For a moment nobody moves.*) I said, off with your rags! Come on, disrobe! Everything off down to your pants.

(*The SLAVES begin to undress and then attire themselves in a motley assortment of second-hand mismatched 'uniforms'; great coats, sailor's jackets, white shirts and hats.*)

(*As they dress.*) In exchange for your service in helping to quell this illegal rebellion by these American subjects of the king, you will be rewarded with your freedom. Do I make myself clear? (*They say nothing.*) I said, do I make myself clear? When I ask you a question you answer either 'yes sir' or 'no sir', so let's try this again. Do I make myself clear?

SLAVES: Yes sir.

REDCOAT: (*To DAVID GEORGE.*) Is this everybody?

DAVID GEORGE: Everybody?

REDCOAT: I am speaking English. I take it you understand English.

DAVID GEORGE: Of course.

REDCOAT: Then you will remember that when I ask a question the correct and proper response is either 'yes sir' or 'no sir', do you understand?

DAVID GEORGE: Yes sir.

REDCOAT: Good, then let's try it again. Is this everybody?

(*THOMAS PETERS begins to walk towards the line of newly uniformed slaves.*)

THOMAS PETERS: No.

(*The REDCOAT turns to face THOMAS PETERS.*)

REDCOAT: 'No'?

THOMAS PETERS: No, this is not everybody.

REDCOAT: If you intend to join your friends then you are late. (*Pause.*) Well, disrobe. What are you waiting for?

(*THOMAS PETERS begins to take off his clothes.*)

DAVID GEORGE: I am happy that you have changed your mind.

THOMAS PETERS: I have not changed my mind.

(*THOMAS PETERS finishes dressing himself in the uniform of the British. He stands with the SLAVES. The REDCOAT examines him closely.*)

REDCOAT: What is your name?

THOMAS PETERS: Thomas.

REDCOAT: Thomas what?

THOMAS PETERS: The man who claims to own me is named Peters.

REDCOAT: Thomas Peters.

THOMAS PETERS: Thomas.

REDCOAT: Thomas Peters. (*THOMAS PETERS says nothing. To the assembled SLAVES.*) This foolish American rebellion has reached a critical stage and so you men shall all see the action of battle within days. And you women shall cook, clean and wash for these soldiers. (*To the MEN.*) However, before you take up the king's arms you must swear the oath of loyalty. Repeat after me. 'I do swear that I enter freely and voluntarily into His Majesty's service…'

SLAVES: 'I do swear that I enter freely and voluntarily into His Majesty's service…'

REDCOAT: '…and I do enlist myself without the least compulsion or persuasion into the Negro Company commanded by Captain Martin…'

SLAVES: '…and I do enlist myself without the least compulsion or persuasion into the Negro Company commanded by Captain Martin…'

REDCOAT: '…and that I will demean myself orderly and faithfully and will cheerfully obey all such directions as I may receive from my said Captain… So help me God.'

SLAVES: '…and that I will demean myself orderly and faithfully and will cheerfully obey all such directions as I may receive from my said Captain… So help me God.'

(*The REDCOAT looks carefully at all the new recruits, but he is particularly interested in THOMAS PETERS, who has not taken the oath with a great deal of enthusiasm. He prods him in the chest.*)

REDCOAT: Step forward soldier. (*THOMAS PETERS takes a step forward.*) Are you cheerful, soldier?

THOMAS PETERS: Cheerful?

REDCOAT: Yes 'happy'. Don't repeat my words, boy. It's our language, we gave it to you. I know what I'm saying. Are you happy?

THOMAS PETERS: I don't know.

REDCOAT: I don't know, sir!

THOMAS PETERS: I don't know, sir.

REDCOAT: (*Laughs.*) You don't seem very happy, but surely you should be. You're about to get your freedom. Repeat after me, this time with some enthusiasm, soldier. As if you're happy. 'I, Thomas Peters, will demean myself orderly and faithfully…' (*THOMAS PETERS says nothing.*) Are you deaf, soldier?

THOMAS PETERS: No sir.

REDCOAT: Then I suggest you obey orders. Immediately!

(*THOMAS PETERS stares directly into the REDCOAT's eyes.*)

THOMAS PETERS: I, Thomas Peters, will demean myself orderly and faithfully…

REDCOAT: ...and will cheerfully obey all such directions as I may receive from my said Captain... So help me God.

THOMAS PETERS: ...and will cheerfully obey all such directions as I may receive from my said Captain...

REDCOAT: ... So help me God.

THOMAS PETERS: ... So help me God.

REDCOAT: You, my boy, may need all of God's help if you don't get rid of your attitude. Do you understand me, soldier? (*Pause.*) Well?

THOMAS PETERS: Yes sir.

REDCOAT: Yes sir! Remember, you're a British soldier now. (*In his face.*) British!

(*We hear the noise of drums and battle in the distance, which grows increasingly loud and furious. The stage goes to black as the sound of battle rises even louder.*)

SCENE FOUR

Lights come up on GRANVILLE SHARP standing alone on stage. He is holding some papers from which he is making a speech. His dress is slightly unkempt and dishevelled, and he is clearly not a natural speaker.

GRANVILLE SHARP: And why do we keep these men in bondage?

VOICE IN AUDIENCE: To stop the blackies running wild.

(*There is laughter. GRANVILLE SHARP consults his notes.*)

GRANVILLE SHARP: They produce something that we all want.

VOICE IN AUDIENCE: Young ones.

(*There is more laughter. Two MEN lug a sack onto the stage and they stand with GRANVILLE SHARP.*)

GRANVILLE SHARP: We are addicted to sugar.

(*The MEN slit open the bag of sugar and pour it onto the stage.*)

VOICE IN AUDIENCE: Here, I'll take a pound of the old Jamaican.

GRANVILLE SHARP: All of us, every last one of us, must learn to boycott this poison and thereby destroy this wicked plantation system which inflicts this bondage on our fellow men.

VOICE IN AUDIENCE: Oi! Scarecrow! Looks like a bit of time out in the sun wouldn't do you no harm.

(*Lights up on two BLACK SOLDIERS and two WHITE SOLDIERS under an American flag, and three BLACK SOLDIERS and one WHITE SOLDIER under a Union Jack. We recognize DAVID GEORGE and THOMAS PETERS as two of the BLACK SOLDIERS under the Union Jack, and the REDCOAT recruiting officer as the WHITE SOLDIER. DAVID GEORGE seems visibly frightened. The SOLDIERS on each side are lined up and they face each other. In a stylized manner, the Americans take one step forward and fire, and the British take one step back.*)

THOMAS PETERS: David George, what does your Bible tell you about killing?

DAVID GEORGE: I cannot hear you.

THOMAS PETERS: (*Laughs.*) Does your book not instruct you that it is sinful to kill your fellow man?

REDCOAT: Peters!

(*The third BLACK SOLDIER is shot and falls to the ground. DAVID GEORGE puts down his rifle and stoops to help the man.*)

THOMAS PETERS: Leave him and fight!

REDCOAT: Pick up your rifle, soldier! (*DAVID GEORGE is unsure what to do. He looks up at THOMAS PETERS and the REDCOAT.*) I'm giving you an order, boy. You're a soldier of the King of England now. Dead men cannot fight.

(*A reluctant DAVID GEORGE picks up his rifle and gets to his feet. The REDCOAT and DAVID GEORGE and THOMAS PETERS make a 'stylized' retreat under fire.*)

(*We are at an auction at a London coffee house. A frightened-looking black MAN stands on a box surrounded by MEN who are ready to bid on him.*)

AUCTIONEER: Well come along then, in this coffee house you know we sell only the finest blacks. And look at him. This is the prime nigger of this or any other day. Freshly loaded at the West India docks, property of Captain George Lewis of the Duke of Gloucester, recently returned from doing business in the Gambia and Barbados.

BIDDER: Twelve guineas.

AUCTIONEER: Do I hear thirteen? (*Points.*) Thirteen over here. Fourteen? (*Points.*) Fourteen. (*Points.*) Fifteen. (*Points.*) Sixteen.

BIDDER: Twenty guineas.

AUCTIONEER: Twenty-one? Come on, look at him, I'll guarantee he's a fine breeder. (*Laughter. Points.*) Twenty-two, over here. (*Points.*) Twenty-three. (*GRANVILLE SHARP steps forward and raises his hand.*)

GRANVILLE SHARP: I bid freedom for Captain Lewis' so-called property. That's my bid. Freedom!

AUCTIONEER: Well, today, Mr Sharp, the price of freedom is twenty-three guineas, but I'll warrant that once again it's beyond your pocket, as appears to be the case every time you come down here disturbing our proceedings.

GRANVILLE SHARP: But this is wrong!

AUCTIONEER: Away with you, sir. Disrupting legal business dealings with your foolish pettiness. Away with you!

(*GRANVILLE SHARP begins to walk off.*)

(*THOMAS PETERS and DAVID GEORGE sit together before a campfire. They both look tired and near exhaustion. The REDCOAT stands over them. He too appears to be fatigued.*)

REDCOAT: The situation is not good, but most of you blacks have fought with courage.

DAVID GEORGE: The situation is not good?

REDCOAT: Soldier, today we retreated. Did you not notice that we gave up considerable ground?

THOMAS PETERS: (*Laughs.*) My colleague is a man of God.

REDCOAT: We are all men of God. At least those of us with souls. Sleep well. We leave before dawn.

(*The REDCOAT leaves them together.*)

THOMAS PETERS: We cannot last much longer.

DAVID GEORGE: Do you think the battle is lost?

THOMAS PETERS: Their battle is lost.

DAVID GEORGE: They have promised to take us to England where we shall be free men. Perhaps it is no bad thing that this war shall soon be concluded.

THOMAS PETERS: And what are we to do in this England?

DAVID GEORGE: We shall be free to be men.

THOMAS PETERS: I beg you, sleep David George. When you awake you will realize that you have been dreaming a foolish dream.

DAVID GEORGE: You believe the British will betray us?

THOMAS PETERS: (*Laughs.*) In America we fight and we kill for them. What use are we to them on the streets of their cities? (*Offers DAVID GEORGE a piece of bread.*) Bread?

DAVID GEORGE: Thomas, my rations are exhausted. I have nothing to offer you in return.

THOMAS PETERS: (*Laughs.*) Then you shall be in my debt. (*DAVID GEORGE hesitates to take the proffered bread.*) Consider it a gift, David George. A gift from an African brother.

(*DAVID GEORGE takes the bread.*)

DAVID GEORGE: Surely some of them are men of honour.

THOMAS PETERS: They are Englishmen, Mr George. Englishmen.

(*GRANVILLE SHARP is standing in the street handing out leaflets to passers-by. A MAN takes one and reads it as he walks off. He stops and returns. He screws the leaflet into a ball and hurls it in GRANVILLE SHARP's face then walks off again. GRANVILLE SHARP hands a leaflet to a WOMAN who smiles then, having glanced at it, shakes her head. A lower-class MAN grabs them all and scatters them to the wind leaving a helpless GRANVILLE SHARP under a paper shower of his own propaganda.*

GRANVILLE SHARP hears a man crying for help. He slowly walks toward him and sees a brutally beaten black MAN lying on the ground and bleeding profusely from the head.)

JAMES SOMERSET: Please sir, my name is James Somerset.

GRANVILLE SHARP: Who has done this to you?

JAMES SOMERSET: My master brought me from Jamaica and used me ill. I ran away but he found me and beat me.

GRANVILLE SHARP: And you have run away again?

JAMES SOMERSET: Please help me, sir. I am a Christian man.

(GRANVILLE SHARP takes off his jacket and begins to staunch the flow of blood.)

GRANVILLE SHARP: No more words, Mr Somerset. I shall help you. Can you stand?

(GRANVILLE SHARP helps him to his feet and begins to escort him off stage.)

(THOMAS PETERS, DAVID GEORGE and the REDCOAT advance one step at a time. Then they stop. They see two WHITE SOLDIERS and two BLACK SOLDIERS under the American flag.)

DAVID GEORGE: *(Points.)* That man, he is from our plantation.

THOMAS PETERS: He was in charge of the horses. His name is William.

DAVID GEORGE: William!

REDCOAT: *(To DAVID GEORGE.)* Shoot him!

DAVID GEORGE: But I know that man.

REDCOAT: I don't care if it's your father, shoot him!

DAVID GEORGE: Shoot him?

(*THOMAS PETERS takes aim and shoots the BLACK SOLDIER dead.*)

I am not a soldier. (*Puts down his rifle.*)

REDCOAT: Pick it up!

DAVID GEORGE: There must be some other way. (*Tears off his military jacket.*) Are we all not children of God?

REDCOAT: We are that, but I'd rather not meet God the Father just yet.

THOMAS PETERS: (*To DAVID GEORGE.*) Pull yourself together! This is no way to behave. Not in front of these people.

DAVID GEORGE: I am sorry, but this killing is not for me. (*Pause.*) I am sorry.

(*ELIZA SHARP appears on stage with a candle. She discovers GRANVILLE SHARP late at night and hard at work at a desk that is piled high with papers. She places the candle on the desk.*)

ELIZA SHARP: Granville, I will not stand by and let you ruin your eyes.

GRANVILLE SHARP: Thank you, but I have sufficient light.

ELIZA SHARP: Look at your clothes, Granville. When was the last time you enjoyed a clean-shirt day?

GRANVILLE SHARP: Eliza, please.

ELIZA SHARP: You labour at these books all hours of the day and night, but to what purpose? The air about you is foul.

GRANVILLE SHARP: But that is it!

ELIZA SHARP: That is what? Tell me, dear brother. Am I in some way responsible for this transformation? Has my teasing affected you to the extent that you abandon your job as a clerk and choose now to campaign full-time for this…this cause.

GRANVILLE SHARP: Eliza, you must in no way feel guilty. My conscience has been stirred in a manner I thought impossible. A man should not be beaten like a dog and deprived of his liberty. For the first time in my life, I am clear about my role in the world. And the intricacies of these legal arguments seem suited to my mind.

ELIZA SHARP: But you are not a lawyer, Granville.

GRANVILLE SHARP: Well, you have said yourself, I have no career, merely a series of temporary concerns.

ELIZA SHARP: And is this not just another temporary concern?

GRANVILLE SHARP: But I am making a contribution. My dear Eliza, the air of England is simply too pure to tolerate slavery. (*Gestures.*) It is too pure! A man has but one life on this earth, that is all. If he is truly fortunate then, within the span of his brief lifetime, there might appear to him some small way in which he might be useful to his fellow man. (*Pause.*) I am blessed, Eliza, for I believe that my present labours are, indeed, useful. I desire neither fame nor fortune. I simply wish to ensure that in England we continue to breathe fresh, pure, air. (*Pause.*) It is truly a small thing, but for me it is everything.

ELIZA SHARP: Everything? Is there not some young lady who might cause your heart to skip a beat?

GRANVILLE SHARP: Such emotions of the heart appear to be lost to me. But what of *your* suitor?

ELIZA SHARP: My what?

GRANVILLE SHARP: Lieutenant Clarkson.

ELIZA SHARP: My dear Granville, surely you make sport with me? You must rest now if you are to be clear-minded in court tomorrow.

GRANVILLE SHARP: Do you deny that he is fond of you?

ELIZA SHARP: Lieutenant Clarkson is a coy, somewhat careful man.

GRANVILLE SHARP: And you seek a man of action?

ELIZA SHARP: I do not seek a man of any kind.

GRANVILLE SHARP: His older brother is a man of fire and indomitable spirit.

ELIZA SHARP: Were Thomas Clarkson the last man on the face of the earth, I would happily embrace spinsterhood.

GRANVILLE SHARP: I feel quite sure than Mr Thomas Clarkson is already aware of the strength of your feelings on this matter.

ELIZA SHARP: Good. Now, it is late, Granville, and you have a most important day ahead of you.

GRANVILLE SHARP: But my dear sister…

ELIZA SHARP: (*Blows out the candle.*) There shall be no further conversation on this subject. Tomorrow, I shall accompany you to court, but tonight you must rest, and that is the end of the matter.

SCENE FIVE

GRANVILLE SHARP is holding a pamphlet and some papers. He stands in an antechamber with a somewhat bemused ELIZA SHARP.

ELIZA SHARP: My dear Granville, surely Lord Chief Justice Mansfield is tired of case after case of kidnapped slaves being set before him.

GRANVILLE SHARP: Then let him accustom himself to fatigue for I intend to press the issue until he makes a ruling outlawing slavery in our country. Today represents a fine chance of such a ruling. The case of poor Mr Somerset is a very strong one.

ELIZA SHARP: But won't they simply send him back to Jamaica with his master?

GRANVILLE SHARP: In England Mr Somerset should have no master. This is the substance of our case. I barely slept a wink last night, rehearsing in my mind each element of the argument. Where is Mr Somerset's lawyer?

ELIZA SHARP: Should he not be here with us for you to give him final instructions? My dear brother, you have been abandoned.

GRANVILLE SHARP: I have always moved in a limited circle, but these days its circumference appears to be shrinking. I am beginning to think of myself as a bore.

ELIZA SHARP: To me you can never be anything less than fascinating. (*Points.*) I take it this is your lawyer?

(*SERGEANT DAVY, in full regalia and wig, is perusing a brief as he enters the antechamber.*)

GRANVILLE SHARP: (*To SERGEANT DAVY.*) Are we ready and prepared for victory?

SERGEANT DAVY: Your optimism is admirable, Mr Sharp, but let us press on to practical matters. Your presence in the courtroom might upset the day.

GRANVILLE SHARP: (*Laughs.*) What is it that the newspapers call me? A self-righteous nonentity who is meddling with the law.

SERGEANT DAVY: But do you agree not to enter the courtroom?

GRANVILLE SHARP: Do these scribblers not understand that we must clean this taint of slavery from our country and then our Empire.

SERGEANT DAVY: Mr Sharp, you waste your words. I do not need to be convinced of the necessity of outlawing slavery. I ask you again, will you remain in the antechamber?

GRANVILLE SHARP: (*Opens his pamphlet.*) I take it you have read my modest book?

SERGEANT DAVY: There is nothing modest about your book. It reveals an outstanding legal mind, but Mr Sharp you are not a lawyer.

ELIZA SHARP: So you would hide my brother in a side room like some spurned dog.

SERGEANT DAVY: Miss Sharp, the Lord Chief Justice is over familiar with the presence of your brother in his courtroom. I do not wish to irritate Judge Mansfield, that is all. The issue here is not pride, but victory.

GRANVILLE SHARP: Mr Davy, the condition of a slave is not, as Chief Justice Mansfield has attempted to argue, comparable to that of an English apprentice. If only he would read my book he would understand his own English law.

SERGEANT DAVY: Mr Sharp, I am sure he has read your book. All concerned with this issue, from both sides, have read your book. But, as you have already surmised, the law, whether English or otherwise, is not always on the side of justice.

GRANVILLE SHARP: But English common law is clear that no person in England shall be regarded as property.

ELIZA SHARP: Then what are we doing here?

SERGEANT DAVY: Young lady, we are once again begging for justice. This time for Mr James Somerset.

GRANVILLE SHARP: If black men can be captives in our land then we are no better than the Turks or the Americans.

ELIZA SHARP: Surely, your Mr Somerset speaks English? Why not let him address the court.

GRANVILLE SHARP: Our appeal has to be to the law. The details of the law are…

ELIZA SHARP: Are what? Beyond the understanding of Mr Somerset?

GRANVILLE SHARP: To some extent, yes.

SERGEANT DAVY: Young lady, perhaps you would like Mr Somerset to remove his shirt and display marks of flagellation? This is an English court of law, and I insist that we argue this case without recourse to the theatrics of Drury Lane. The negro shall remain silent. Should we not receive a favourable judgement, then I truly fear for the future of the African man in England. In fact, without the protection of English law his only choice would be a return home to Africa.

ELIZA SHARP: And would that be a terrible fate?

GRANVILLE SHARP: Do we send the Frenchman back to France, or the Spaniard back to Spain? Once they are in this country then English law extends to them.

(*We hear the judicial knock of the hammer. Lights up on LORD CHIEF JUSTICE MANSFIELD. He is flanked by three grim-faced ASSOCIATE JUSTICES.*)

SERGEANT DAVY: Mr Sharp?

GRANVILLE SHARP: You truly wish to exclude me from the courtroom? (*Pause. There is no answer.*) I understand. I shall await the judgement.

ELIZA SHARP: Granville, shall we walk abroad a while? I promised Lieutenant Clarkson that we might rendezvous with him.

SERGEANT DAVY: Mr Sharp.

GRANVILLE SHARP: A moment, Eliza.

SERGEANT DAVY: Mr Sharp, please remember, you have already affected a great number of English minds. If Lord Chief Justice Mansfield chooses not to outlaw slavery then you must not take it to heart.

(*SERGEANT DAVY moves toward the LORD CHIEF JUSTICE MANSFIELD and his ASSOCIATES.*)

ELIZA SHARP: (*To GRANVILLE SHARP.*) Do you intend to remain here, like an unwelcome guest at the ball?

GRANVILLE SHARP: I shall listen to the judgement from this vantage point.

(*The light tightens on MANSFIELD who, in a lilting, but somewhat hesitant, Perthshire accent begins to deliver his verdict. We focus on GRANVILLE SHARP, who reacts to the nuances of MANSFIELD's speech. ELIZA SHARP tries to comfort him when necessary.*)

LORD CHIEF JUSTICE MANSFIELD: The question before me today, a question that I will admit has been debated with some admirable vigour, is not some great and general issue, although the throngs gathered hereabouts would seem to believe so, rather it is the question of whether there is sufficient cause for the return of the man known as James Somerset to the Americas which implies that the man who claims to be his owner is therefore the victim of an unlawful act as efforts have been made by many people to avoid the transportation of James Somerset out of these lands and in the direction of the Americas. In short, the owner has been unable to export his property. I have already rehearsed at length my belief that in law, neither the fact that a slave has entered England, and much less the issue of whether that slave has been baptised or not, can be held up as evidence to thereafter reduce the rights of masters to naught. And yet... (*MANSFIELD pauses and looks up from his papers before him.*) ...and yet while slavery has been many things in different ages and states, the exercise of the power of a master over his slave must be supported by the laws of particular countries. It thereby follows that no foreigner can in England claim such a right over a man. Such a claim is not known to the laws of England, and the power claimed was never in use here or acknowledged by the law of this land. A return in such circumstances cannot be approved of by the laws of this kingdom therefore the man cannot be transported and must be free to remain in England.

(*The judicial hammer knocks three times as LORD CHIEF JUSTICE MANSFIELD and his three ASSOCIATES rise and begin to leave the courtroom. SERGEANT DAVY smiles broadly. MANSFIELD leaves the stage. A flute and drum begin to mark a beat, and joyous BLACKS appear and begin to celebrate and dance. ELIZA and GRANVILLE SHARP are joined by JOHN CLARKSON. The three of them look on and watch for a few moments.*)

GRANVILLE SHARP: (*To JOHN CLARKSON.*) I apologize for the noise and great inconvenience of the negroes. Today is a day that many have waited for, and I suppose they cannot help but besport themselves with a kind of reckless abandon.

JOHN CLARKSON: There is certainly great spirit to their exuberance.

ELIZA SHARP: If they wish to stay in England they must, however, adjust to our customs. Their negro frolics are unseemly.

GRANVILLE SHARP: Have you not seen the lower orders of our own complexion behaving with far less decorum. Brawling and setting about each other like wild animals.

ELIZA SHARP: But this negro merriment, while amusing, is of a type that is unquestionably not English. But Granville you must rest now. You have secured your victory, yet your mind remains over-employed. Perhaps you might learn to sing and jig about? (*To JOHN CLARKSON.*) Can you teach my brother to dance?

JOHN CLARKSON: Dance?

GRANVILLE SHARP: But this is not a true victory. Lord Chief Justice Mansfield has not stated that it is illegal to hold a slave in England, he has only ruled that it is illegal to transport a man against his will. Transportation, not ownership, is the issue that has been decided upon.

ELIZA SHARP: And do you intend to inform our negro friends that they are mistaken in their revelry?

JOHN CLARKSON: Surely these blacks are therefore in some danger?

ELIZA SHARP: They seem quite content.

GRANVILLE SHARP: They are happy, but I fear that their happiness might be short-lived. Perhaps we might return them to an Africa which might well be kinder to them.

ELIZA SHARP: Transportation?

GRANVILLE SHARP: Perhaps the establishment of some form of trading colony.

JOHN CLARKSON: You wish these people to leave England?

GRANVILLE SHARP: Despite all of our efforts, the people of this country still appear to be indifferent to the plight of our negroes.

ELIZA SHARP: And so you propose shipping them out of our kingdom?

GRANVILLE SHARP: I am merely thinking aloud. But you said yourself that there were too many of them in our land. Would you have them remain in a place that is not yet ready to welcome them as free men and women?

JOHN CLARKSON: But to abandon them to some sort of African trading post?

ELIZA SHARP: It appears that my brother is now ready to compromise.

GRANVILLE SHARP: Eliza, there is no compromise! (*The BLACKS stop dancing and singing. They look at the gathered group.*) What say you Lieutenant Clarkson?

JOHN CLARKSON: I am for liberty and freedom.

GRANVILLE SHARP: Indeed, we are British not American.

ELIZA SHARP: Come. Enough words. Let us dance.

(*GRANVILLE SHARP and JOHN CLARKSON are reluctant.*)

Well, are these basic steps beyond your comprehension?

(*ELIZA SHARP begins to dance, much to the amusement of the BLACKS. GRANVILLE SHARP and JOHN CLARKSON join her, but they are hopelessly out of step and rhythm. The BLACKS continue to be amused.*)

SCENE SIX

DAVID GEORGE carries a crystal decanter of sherry on a tray with two glasses. He crosses towards GENERAL LORD CHARLES CORNWALLIS, the commander of British troops in America, who is standing over a map. A young LIEUTENANT stands with him and he also scrutinizes the map. We can hear gunfire in the distance.

DAVID GEORGE: Your sherry, sir.

CORNWALLIS: Yes, yes, of course. Well, what are you waiting for, just pour it.

DAVID GEORGE: Two glasses, sir?

CORNWALLIS: Well don't you see two men before you? Good Lord, it appears that you are no better as a valet than you were as a soldier.

LIEUTENANT: The Americans have effectively cut off any chance of our receiving supplies from the land to the west.

CORNWALLIS: This is a damn big country, there must be some nook or cranny through which we can still replenish the men?

LIEUTENANT: It would appear not, sir. (*He takes his sherry from DAVID GEORGE.*) Thank you.

(*DAVID GEORGE retreats and stands by the door. The LIEUTENANT proposes a toast.*)

To your good health Lord Cornwallis.

CORNWALLIS: Are you being deliberately facetious, young man?

LIEUTENANT: No, sir. I mean it, sir. I wish you all the best.

CORNWALLIS: This campaign is lost if we don't find a way to break out of Yorktown. They've cut off supplies to the sea in the east, and now you tell me it is hopeless to the west. Bugger my health, the health of the kingdom lies in the balance. We cannot afford to lose this American colony. Not to these second-rate brewers and farmers.

(*A British OFFICER enters. He hands the LIEUTENANT a note which he starts to read.*)

LIEUTENANT: I must tell you, sir, there is one such second-rate man who seeks an audience with you.

CORNWALLIS: An American?

LIEUTENANT: A representative of those people. He claims to have a proposal.

CORNWALLIS: He wishes to make a proposal? To me?

LIEUTENANT: You are our commanding officer, sir.

CORNWALLIS: Thank you, Lieutenant. I am perfectly aware of who I am. (*Pause.*) Well show him in then.

(*The LIEUTENANT signals to the OFFICER, who leaves and then immediately returns with an AMERICAN OFFICER. Having done so the OFFICER once again withdraws.*)

AMERICAN OFFICER: Lord Cornwallis, an honour and a privilege, sir.

CORNWALLIS: And to what do I owe the pleasure of your company?

AMERICAN OFFICER: Your situation is lost, sir.

CORNWALLIS: And your impertinence would appear to respect no boundaries. My lieutenant claims you have a proposal. I will extend you the courtesy of listening to whatever you might have to say on this matter. I do not, however, have any interest in your assessment of His Majesty's military situation. Am I making myself clear?

AMERICAN OFFICER: I understand.

CORNWALLIS: Well, out with it, man. Do you, or do you not, have a proposal?

AMERICAN OFFICER: Return our blacks to us.

CORNWALLIS: Your blacks?

AMERICAN OFFICER: You have no further use for them.

CORNWALLIS: Are you issuing me an order?

AMERICAN OFFICER: We shall return them to work on the land.

CORNWALLIS: In chains?

AMERICAN OFFICER: You know the truth of their situation. Compared to their heathen life in Africa, this is a blessed liberty. There will be no ill-usage.

CORNWALLIS: Lieutenant, you may escort the officer from my tent. (*Turns his back on the AMERICAN OFFICER.*)

AMERICAN OFFICER: With all due respect, sir, the blacks are our property. They belong to us.

LIEUTENANT: (*Approaches the AMERICAN OFFICER.*) You must leave now.

AMERICAN OFFICER: (*To LIEUTENANT.*) I warn you against placing a hand on my person. (*To CORNWALLIS.*) Our blacks have served their purpose, and you and I both know that they are now more trouble to you than they are worth. I offer you a solution. In friendship.

(*The AMERICAN OFFICER waits, but CORNWALLIS says nothing in reply.*)

(*Moves to leave.*) Your sentimentality surprises me, sir. Good day.

(*The AMERICAN OFFICER leaves CORNWALLIS and the LIEUTENANT alone together.*)

LIEUTENANT: Might I make a suggestion, sir?

CORNWALLIS: You know he's right. We should perhaps expel the blacks? It was an absurd desperation to recruit them in the first place.

LIEUTENANT: Sir?

CORNWALLIS: Well, are we not short of supplies? They eat and drink our food, don't they? If we get rid of them then perhaps we can hold out until reinforcements arrive.

LIEUTENANT: But we are not...

CORNWALLIS: We are not what, Lieutenant?

LIEUTENANT: Not barbarians, sir. These men fought and died for us, and some did so with great distinction. Even as we speak one of them is waiting outside, sir, for an audience. You are to decorate him for bravery.

CORNWALLIS: Bravery?

LIEUTENANT: Yes sir, bravery. We would have faced defeat before now if it were not for our negro recruits.

CORNWALLIS: And your suggestion?

LIEUTENANT: I think Your Lordship understands that we must retreat or face disaster.

CORNWALLIS: Lieutenant, I am aware that the war is finished and we cannot remain here. It will simply take me a little while to adjust my mind to this reality. In the meantime, I thought we were talking about the blacks. What do you suggest we do about the blacks?

LIEUTENANT: Sir, let the able-bodied blacks and their families remain with our men as we retreat and make our way north to New York.

CORNWALLIS: Retreat?

LIEUTENANT: You said it yourself, sir. We cannot remain here.

CORNWALLIS: And the reinforcements?

LIEUTENANT: It will be too late, sir.

CORNWALLIS: So you propose taking all the blacks?

LIEUTENANT: I am afraid some are not healthy enough. They must be left behind.

CORNWALLIS: To die?

LIEUTENANT: Sir, we must take as many with us as possible. It is our duty.

CORNWALLIS: Retreat, eh?

LIEUTENANT: I am sorry.

(*CORNWALLIS sits heavily.*)

CORNWALLIS: Leave me.

LIEUTENANT: Yes, of course, sir.

CORNWALLIS: Lieutenant.

LIEUTENANT: Yes, sir.

CORNWALLIS: You are not proposing that we take them to England?

LIEUTENANT: No sir. Just somewhere safe. We could eventually ship them to a place beyond New York.

CORNWALLIS: Yes, we could do that, I suppose.

LIEUTENANT: I think so, sir. Nova Scotia, perhaps. We own the property, and despite its harsh climate there is land there that is available to be cultivated.

CORNWALLIS: I see. But not England?

LIEUTENANT: England is *our* home. What would they do there?

CORNWALLIS: Quite. (*Pause.*) You may leave now, Lieutenant.

LIEUTENANT: Thank you, sir.

(*The LIEUTENANT begins to back out of the room. He sees DAVID GEORGE, who has been listening. However, he says nothing to him. He simply leaves. DAVID GEORGE approaches CORNWALLIS.*)

DAVID GEORGE: Lord Cornwallis, sir?

CORNWALLIS: I am sorry, David. (*Pause.*) I didn't see you there.

DAVID GEORGE: Will there be anything else, sir? (*Pause.*) Thomas Peters, sir?

CORNWALLIS: Who?

DAVID GEORGE: A medal, sir. For bravery on the field of battle.

CORNWALLIS: For heaven's sake, man. Not now. Another time.

DAVID GEORGE: He has been waiting, sir.

CORNWALLIS: Away with you, man!

(*He waves DAVID GEORGE away. DAVID GEORGE moves off. He stops opposite THOMAS PETERS, who is waiting to receive his decoration.*)

DAVID GEORGE: The commanding officer is occupied.

THOMAS PETERS: Occupied?

DAVID GEORGE: His situation is perplexing.

THOMAS PETERS: *His* situation?

(*THOMAS PETERS slowly takes off his British soldier's jacket and crumples it into a ball. He throws it on the ground in disgust.*)

DAVID GEORGE: We are to retreat. To New York.

(*Other BLACKS begin to gather on stage. They are joined by WHITE REDCOATS. Everybody begins slowly to move.*)

THOMAS PETERS: To New York?

DAVID GEORGE: And then beyond.

(*The WHITES stop moving and the BLACKS continue to inch forward. THOMAS PETERS and DAVID GEORGE are joined by their wives, PHYLLIS and a heavily pregnant SALLY, and by ISAAC.*)

THOMAS PETERS: To where?

DAVID GEORGE: Nova Scotia. Apparently there is land there that we might cultivate and own.

THOMAS PETERS: I am not going to Nova Scotia.

DAVID GEORGE: Then where are you going, Thomas? Is this where you abandon us?

THOMAS PETERS: You dare talk to me of abandonment? You who encouraged this stupidity?

ISAAC: Thomas Peters has never trusted an Englishman. He always warned us against the British.

SALLY PETERS: We must go with them, Thomas. If we remain here we will be recaptured. Do you wish your child to be born into slavery?

ISAAC: (*To THOMAS PETERS.*) Wherever we go, you must lead us?

SALLY PETERS: Thomas, we cannot go back to slavery.

THOMAS PETERS: I will not lead you to Nova Scotia.

DAVID GEORGE: Then follow. But, Thomas, do not place yourself and your wife in this danger. I beg you, come with us.

PHYLLIS GEORGE: David, we must go.

THOMAS PETERS: Look to your wife.

DAVID GEORGE: Isaac?

ISAAC: And you say we shall be landowners in this Nova Scotia?

THOMAS PETERS: Let us go to this place and find out if Mr George is once again deceiving us.

SALLY PETERS: Thank you, Thomas.

(*THOMAS PETERS and DAVID GEORGE stare at each other. The group of BLACKS begins to trudge aimlessly on. DAVID GEORGE breaks eye contact and turns and joins them. THOMAS PETERS, SALLY PETERS and ISAAC follow.*)

SCENE SEVEN

We are at a public meeting. On the platform is a long wooden table and seated behind the table are GRANVILLE SHARP, THOMAS CLARKSON, JOHN CLARKSON, ELIZA SHARP and HENRY DE MANE, a black former slave. On the wall behind them is an image of the Brookes slave ship, with the slaves packed together tightly – like logs. There is also an image of the pleading, kneeling negro with the inscription, 'Am I not a man and a brother?' THOMAS CLARKSON speaks directly to the audience.

THOMAS CLARKSON: I believe that Mr Sharp has a few more words which he wishes to address to you all.

(*GRANVILLE SHARP climbs to his feet and begins to speak slowly, but with passion.*)

GRANVILLE SHARP: For these past few days my colleagues and I gathered hereabouts have been travelling England in an attempt to do what? To make you good people aware of the evil that we Englishmen are tolerating both overseas and here in our own land. Who among us would wish to live as a slave? Denied liberty. Denied freedom. Incapable of shaping the destiny of one's own family. Well? (*He waits for a response from the audience, but there is silence.*) None of us would wish to embrace such a life. (*He turns to HENRY DE MANE.*) Mr De Mane, please stand up. (*DE MANE rises to his feet.*) This man was formerly a slave. Used,

no, abused would be a more appropriate term. Abused
in Barbados for many years, having previously been
snatched from his native Africa. When his master came to
England he brought Henry as an ornament, if you will. He
displayed the poor man in finery and silks like an exhibit
at Bartholomew Fair. Henry worked for his master but, as
was the case in Barbados, he received neither reward nor
consideration for his labour. But when Henry decided to
seek his liberty and escape the tyranny that had ensnared
his life, and breathe the pure, clean air of England beyond
the jurisdiction of his master, Henry was hunted down like
a dog and captured and beaten. (*He turns to HENRY.*) Henry.
(*HENRY DE MANE removes his jacket and shirt, then he turns his
back to the audience so that the scars and welts and bruises are
all clearly visible. There is a communal gasp at the evidence of the
brutality. GRANVILLE SHARP points to the banner.*) Read the
words. 'Am I not a man and a brother?' Does any person
here doubt that Henry De Mane is both a man – and a
fine man I might add – and our brother in Christ? (*To
HENRY.*) Henry you may replace your shirt. Thank you.
(*To audience.*) The recent case of James Somerset went
some distance towards clarifying the status of these people
among us, but they still live in danger. This is why we are
collecting contributions for the establishment of a Province
of Freedom on the grain coast of Africa. This will be a
place to which the London blacks can voluntarily return
and live peacefully under the jurisdiction of a trading
company which will be based in London. In this way
the blacks can cultivate crops and export their produce
back to London and eventually become a self-sustaining
community. We need funds urgently, for the first ship will
be ready to sail for the grain coast within a month, and
provisions must still be purchased and stores and supplies
laid down in order that our intrepid pioneers might survive
their first African rainy season. (*Pause.*) I see a hand raised
in our audience. Yes, sir.

VOICE: Honourable sirs. Do these blacks truly wish to return
to depravity?

GRANVILLE SHARP: Perhaps Mr De Mane would like to address the question?

THOMAS CLARKSON: I am not sure that will be necessary. Mr De Mane is a farmer who is eager to reclaim the peaceful life that he lost many years past.

ELIZA SHARP: (*To THOMAS CLARKSON in disbelief.*) This man is a farmer?

HENRY DE MANE: I wish to go to Africa where I can be free.

ELIZA SHARP: (*To THOMAS CLARKSON.*) Are these *your* words, Mr Clarkson?

GRANVILLE SHARP: Eliza, please!

THOMAS CLARKSON: No, no, Mr Sharp. A dissenting voice is no bad thing. We appear before the good people of Lincoln in open and free debate on this vexed and complicated issue. I pray, sir, let Miss Sharp take the floor if she so wishes.

ELIZA SHARP: Thank you, sir, but I am happy to know my place.

VOICE: What I want to know is who let these blacks into England in the first place?

GRANVILLE SHARP: (*To audience.*) Perhaps we should confine our discussion to the Province of Freedom. Lieutenant Clarkson. Would you like to add some words?

JOHN CLARKSON: On the subject of the establishing of a province in Africa, I respectfully urge caution. The planning must be thorough and the conditions of transport humane. All of this will require a not inconsiderable amount of money.

THOMAS CLARKSON: Which is precisely why we appear before the good people assembled here. (*JOHN CLARKSON stares at THOMAS CLARKSON.*) Well, my dear brother, you may continue.

JOHN CLARKSON: Shelters will have to be built, and treaties drawn up with the local chiefs to negotiate for land. I am led to believe that some London blacks are suspicious of the motives behind this new province and do not wish to go, especially as the province is to be located in a zone still preyed upon by the slaving ships of Europe.

THOMAS CLARKSON: Yet there are many who *do* wish to leave, such as Mr Henry De Mane here.

ELIZA SHARP: And do you imagine this *farmer* to be of the right character for such a project?

THOMAS CLARKSON: Character?

ELIZA SHARP: Do you believe there to be no degree of person or personality in the ranks of black men?

THOMAS CLARKSON: I am not sure I know Mr De Mane well enough to 'endorse' his character.

ELIZA SHARP: After ten days of travelling the length of England with him you are still unable to form any judgement of his character?

VOICE: Will Mr De Mane be sailing to the Province?

GRANVILLE SHARP: Indeed he will.

VOICE: Good, he looks like a mean brute. (*Laughter.*)

THOMAS CLARKSON: While Mr De Mane escorts the collection plate on a final circumnavigation of the room, a concluding word from Mr Sharp?

(*HENRY DE MANE takes up the collection plate and leaves the platform.*)

GRANVILLE SHARP: To those of you residing outside of our great capital, it is perhaps difficult for you to imagine the scene of hundreds of destitute poor blacks occupying the lowest grades of our society, and thronging about the streets without any confidence of their place in English life. Well such is the scene that would greet you were you to travel to London, and there is every possibility that the poignancy of what would appear before your eyes would break your heart as it daily breaks my own. These people deserve a home. Many of them have given great service on behalf of English masters.

VOICE: I am not an English master.

VOICE: Nor me. I work as hard as any black man. Why do you want to give the blackies special treatment?

GRANVILLE SHARP: But sir, you are at home are you not? And whatever difficulties you may suffer you have the blessed benefit of knowing that you walk tall as a man in a land that you recognize, and among a people who recognize you.

VOICE: So the black man can never be at home in England, is that what you are saying?

THOMAS CLARKSON: What Mr Sharp is trying to say is that at this present time it may well be difficult for the blacks to establish a home in England. This being the case why not found a free and Christian community in Africa to which those who choose to can freely return.

VOICE: And you want money from us?

THOMAS CLARKSON: From those who are able, yes.

VOICE: This smartly dressed darkie down here with the collection plate, he don't look like he be needing much help from the likes of us. (*There is laughter from the audience.*) I wouldn't mind a jacket like his.

JOHN CLARKSON: Then you must work and earn it.

ELIZA SHARP: Well spoken, Lieutenant Clarkson.

JOHN CLARKSON: The streets of London are full of black men who are not able to attire themselves like Mr De Mane. If some among these men would like to roll the dice and seek their fortune overseas, then we must not be derelict in our duty to provide the best possible conditions for them.

THOMAS CLARKSON: Thank you, Lieutenant. Mr Sharp?

GRANVILLE SHARP: I believe there are sufficient negroes in both numbers and capacities to make this trading enterprise a great success. And, of course, the more successful it is, the more evidence we will have to present to those who continue to argue that the negro's position in society is that of a slave perpetually beneath the heel of a white master. Thank you, Mr Clarkson, and thank you to the good people of Lincoln.

(*The speakers at the table get to their feet and begin to disperse. The meeting is over.*)

ELIZA SHARP: (*To THOMAS CLARKSON.*) Are you not proud of your brother? He spoke to the issue.

THOMAS CLARKSON: And in your opinion we spoke to what?

ELIZA SHARP: The good Lieutenant reminds us that Africa is a place of disease and great danger. We are not dispatching these men across the channel to Normandy.

(*GRANVILLE SHARP takes the collection plate from HENRY DE MANE, who quickly leaves.*)

GRANVILLE SHARP: I suspect that once again we have barely covered our expenses.

JOHN CLARKSON: Mr De Mane moves as though late for an appointment.

ELIZA SHARP: Does Mr De Mane have some special talent for making money disappear?

THOMAS CLARKSON: Mr De Mane is no doubt already in pursuit of some pretty country girl.

ELIZA SHARP: (*Stares at the collection plate.*) It is increasingly clear how he obtains the money to purchase his ostentatious clothing.

GRANVILLE SHARP: We must not be too hasty to pass judgement. I believe Henry to be a fine and honourable man.

JOHN CLARKSON: Such a man is not suited to be in the Province of Freedom. A community cannot tolerate theft of any kind.

ELIZA SHARP: Why Lieutenant Clarkson, it appears you are a man of firm convictions.

JOHN CLARKSON: I am afraid there will be no more meetings for me. I shall be seeking a new naval command.

ELIZA SHARP: You are leaving us, Lieutenant Clarkson? How disappointing.

THOMAS CLARKSON: (*To JOHN CLARKSON.*) Brother John, you appear to be distracted.

JOHN CLARKSON: This foolish collection plate is not to my liking. But I am concerned by this whole process. A self-sustaining community requires great planning. Merely transporting men to a place that is out of sight is…is worrisome. These men possess souls; they have feelings and families – perhaps I should see to my own affairs.

THOMAS CLARKSON: And you would abandon Miss Sharp, too?

ELIZA SHARP: (*To THOMAS CLARKSON.*) Your brother can never abandon me, Mr Clarkson. I am neither shackled to him, nor to any other man.

SCENE EIGHT

Lights up on THOMAS PETERS, who stands alone digging a shallow hole. He works in deep solitary concentration. As he does so we see his wife SALLY PETERS being led and supported by ISAAC towards what we now realize is a grave. Beside her walks DAVID GEORGE with a copy of the Bible in his hands. He looks weak, and he stands with the assistance of his wife, PHYLLIS. Other BLACK LOYALISTS gather around. As they do so THOMAS PETERS stops digging. He reaches down and picks up a small bundle wrapped in a white cloth. He slowly leans forward and places the bundle in the grave. SALLY PETERS has to be comforted. THOMAS PETERS begins now to cover the bundle of white cloth with a few shovelfuls of earth. He then casts the shovel to one side and visibly struggles to contain his emotions. He is both upset and angry and he goes to SALLY. ISAAC begins to complete the task of shoveling the earth over the body. DAVID GEORGE steps forward. His voice is weak.

DAVID GEORGE: Dear Lord, we commit to you the body of this small child, Clara, daughter of Thomas and Sally Peters, who has perished from malnutrition here in this harsh and inhospitable climate of Nova Scotia on this 14th day of January, so help me God. Please show mercy on the gentle soul of this innocent child, and welcome her to your bosom now that her life has been so cruelly snatched from her in this wilderness in which we appear to have been cast adrift by the British. (*Pause.*) Thank you, Lord.

PHYLLIS GEORGE: Thomas. Sally. David and I are so sorry. We are here to share your pain with you.

THOMAS PETERS: Have you lost a child? Do you know what it is to lose a child?

SALLY PETERS: Thomas, please.

THOMAS PETERS: (*To DAVID GEORGE.*) You claimed the British would treat us with respect and guarantee our freedom. But when victory eluded these redcoats we were gathered together as cattle and shipped to this place with false promises of seeds, tools, lumber and land. Mr George, we have been abandoned to sleep in tents and crude huts. Diseases carry off the unfortunate, including my own daughter. What have you to say to this?

DAVID GEORGE: We have been betrayed.

THOMAS PETERS: And where are your precious redcoats now?

DAVID GEORGE: Thomas, you speak to me as though I am not also a victim of this wretchedness. Is it fair and reasonable to saddle me with the responsibility for the behaviour of the British?

THOMAS PETERS: Who is responsible for the death of my daughter?

SALLY PETERS: Thomas, please. Clara is gone. She is with the Lord now.

THOMAS PETERS: She is with who? What did you say, Sally?

(*SALLY PETERS averts her eyes and will not respond.*)

DAVID GEORGE: Perhaps a few words about the short, but blessed, life of Clara Peters. She gave joy to two wonderful people, and this gift of happiness is something of a miracle in the circumstances that we are presently being asked to endure. There are verses in the Bible which speak to…

THOMAS PETERS: (*Snatches the Bible from DAVID GEORGE.*) Enough! (*He hurls the Bible into the distance.*) I will hear no more from you or your God. No more! What has your God done for my poor daughter?

DAVID GEORGE: Thomas…

THOMAS PETERS: (*To DAVID GEORGE.*) Do not trouble me with your foolish words.

DAVID GEORGE: Thomas, surely you would rather die as a free man here in this strange, wild Nova Scotia, than be a slave in America?

THOMAS PETERS: I have never been a slave. Even when the white man called me a slave I was free. That is the difference between us! And you ask me where I would rather die? When my time comes you can forget your precious England. I want to feel African soil beneath my feet and see an African sky above my head. I want to be at home, but Africa is not your home is it?

ISAAC: (*To DAVID GEORGE.*) We are African people. Those like yourself who were born in America, you must never forget that you are still an African.

DAVID GEORGE: I too wish to find a place that I might call home, but like you I am tired. Why squabble among ourselves? (*The LOYALISTS begin to grow agitated. To those gathered.*) Please, a little patience.

PHYLLIS GEORGE: David, we are dying in such numbers. (*There is a general chorus of agreement with PHYLLIS GEORGE.*) My husband, I love, respect, and honour you, but how much longer can we survive in this place?

DAVID GEORGE: But my dear Phyllis, people die in Africa too. We must endure whatever trial the good Lord chooses to test our faith.

(*SALLY PETERS collapses in grief. THOMAS PETERS picks her up and cradles her gently in his arms.*)

Is Sally alright?

PHYLLIS GEORGE: David, she has just lost her only child.

THOMAS PETERS: I am a man, not an object to be cast aside once somebody has determined that I am of no further use to him. I will make this white man keep his promises. If it kills me, I will make him respect the black man.

ISAAC: Do you have a plan?

THOMAS PETERS: I have my knowledge that I am right. (*To DAVID GEORGE.*) Where is your God in this land?

DAVID GEORGE: My God is with me, here in my heart.

SALLY PETERS: Thomas, please do not leave me.

DAVID GEORGE: What do you have in mind, Thomas?

SALLY PETERS: You must not travel to England, Thomas. If you leave I shall never see you again.

THOMAS PETERS: I shall do what I have to do in order to make these white people listen.

SALLY PETERS: Are you ready to make a widow of me, Thomas?

THOMAS PETERS: I shall return, Sally. I promise you, I shall return.

(*We hear a loud volley of gunfire and much shouting. Out of the darkness a smartly uniformed HENRY DE MANE appears carrying a musket. He is accompanied by the African chief KING JIMMY and his ATTENDANTS, who carry guns and burning torches. Before him is a dishevelled SETTLER, whom he addresses. The SETTLER seems exhausted, but determined.*).

HENRY DE MANE: There is no God in this land. Only Henry De Mane. (*The SETTLER looks at him, but says nothing.*) Together with this African King Jimmy, I govern this Province of Freedom here in Sierra Leone. You shall obey me or this settlement will be no more. I will simply instruct these African people to burn it to the ground.

SETTLER: Mr De Mane, we all suffered on the journey from England, but now you would truly destroy what little shelter we have established?

HENRY DE MANE: You people are my subjects.

SETTLER: We owe you no allegiance! We are subjects of the King of England and we report to the trading company who sent us here.

HENRY DE MANE: (*Laughs.*) Sent you here for what? To rid themselves of your presence in England and to make money for themselves. The low-class white men who accompanied us to this Province of Freedom have already succumbed to disease. Do you see any others coming to replace them?

SETTLER: And who appointed you to lead us?

HENRY DE MANE: Since the death of the last Englishman have I not negotiated with the local people with your best interests in mind?

SETTLER: Last night three more of our people disappeared. (*Points.*) These Africans dragged them away. Where are our colleagues?

HENRY DE MANE: Have you no respect for these men? They are not merely 'these Africans'. These men are our brothers, and together with them we can build a new community.

SETTLER: No, *my* brothers were dragged away in the middle of the night and you and these Africans sold them to slave traders. We are not stupid, Mr De Mane.

HENRY DE MANE: You accuse me of trading in slaves?

SETTLER: We do not want you as our leader.

HENRY DE MANE: But I am offering you a future. We can work together with this King Jimmy and grow crops, and raise animals.

SETTLER: You will sell more of us as slaves.

HENRY DE MANE: I will trade only those who break my rules! (*Pause.*) Well, do you accept me as your leader?

SETTLER: We came to this place with white men who had been sentenced to hang at Newgate, but these common people are no more and we have survived. Mr De Mane, we have no desire to return to London and be mocked as 'blackbirds'. We no longer wish to be Thames bargemen or beggars on the streets of that city. We shall risk this climate and submit to our fate as free men.

HENRY DE MANE: (*Takes a step towards the SETTLER.*) I like your spirit. I can train you in the slavery business. We shall trade only the weak and infirm. The others we shall protect.

SETTLER: I should spit in your face.

HENRY DE MANE: In one day as a slaver you will earn twice what you might earn in one year planting crops. Can you not see the logic in this?

SETTLER: You sicken me, De Mane.

HENRY DE MANE: If this is your answer then you leave me with little choice. (*He motions to the darkness.*) Come forward. (*Three English SLAVE TRADERS with guns and chains emerge from the bush. They surround the SETTLER and begin to chain him.*) Having recently survived a difficult sea passage, another will not trouble you. (*In the distance we see the glow of burning. The sky is red and flickering. He points.*) There is your Province of Freedom. See how it burns.

SETTLER: May you rot in hell, De Mane.

HENRY DE MANE: (*Laughs.*) I have already done so, and it is called England.

SETTLER: And so now you will sell us? You will take money in exchange for our bodies, and then do what?

HENRY DE MANE: (*Laughs.*) Live as an African, of course. As a king among these fine people.

(*HENRY DE MANE signals to the SLAVE TRADERS to begin to escort the SETTLER away. They push and prod at him as they march off. In the distance the settlement burns.*)

SCENE NINE

It is late at night in GRANVILLE SHARP's modestly furnished study.
A disconcerted GRANVILLE SHARP sits with ELIZA SHARP. A newly
arrived JOHN CLARKSON is dressed in naval uniform. He takes a seat.
An English SERVANT pours tea for GRANVILLE and ELIZA SHARP and
wine for JOHN CLARKSON. Having done so he stands to one side.

JOHN CLARKSON: My brother is away on business in
    Madeira, but he has no doubt already received news of
    the destruction of the Province of Freedom. (*To GRANVILLE
    SHARP.*) I am terribly sorry.

GRANVILLE SHARP: It is difficult to comprehend how this
    disaster could have occurred.

ELIZA SHARP: (*To JOHN CLARKSON.*) Since receiving the news
    Granville has been afflicted with a powerful melancholy.

GRANVILLE SHARP: It appears that a great many lives
    have been lost in this unseemly anarchy. I simply don't
    understand; these men sailed with papers of freedom,
    and we supplied English artisans to assist them. And why
    would Henry behave in this manner?

JOHN CLARKSON: Unfortunately, the whole enterprise
    appears to have concluded in failure.

GRANVILLE SHARP: The Africans burned down the
    settlement, then killed Henry, and they sold the surviving
    settlers into slavery.

ELIZA SHARP: Did Lieutenant Clarkson not suggest that better
    preparations were necessary?

GRANVILLE SHARP: My dear Eliza, is there any purpose to
    this promotion of your intended?

ELIZA SHARP: My intended?

GRANVILLE SHARP: Far be it from me to speculate, but…

ELIZA SHARP: Indeed, it is not for you to speculate!

GRANVILLE SHARP: I am sorry, I did not mean to pry. Forgive
    me.

ELIZA SHARP: You are, of course, forgiven. (*Pause.*) But what now, Granville? News travels, and bad news travels quickly. Surely there is no longer a single black man, woman, or child in England who would willingly clamber aboard one of your vessels.

GRANVILLE SHARP: But there must be some cooling of this antagonism between black and white in England if we are to win the support of the public and abolish slavery.

ELIZA SHARP: So you will once again attempt to transport the black problem overseas in order to pave the way for your legislative glory?

GRANVILLE SHARP: Legislative justice! That is what we seek, justice.

JOHN CLARKSON: I have a ship at my disposal, and some ideas as to how one might establish a society in Africa that is founded upon principles of human need, mutual compassion, and Christian industry. I have no desire to service either commercial or legislative convenience, but I do have a belief that a society founded upon equality might well work.

GRANVILLE SHARP: I take it you have shared your feelings with your brother?

JOHN CLARKSON: My brother is perfectly well aware of my growing unease with his belief in free trading as a remedy to social problems.

ELIZA SHARP: So you are leaving us, Lieutenant Clarkson?

JOHN CLARKSON: Surely there must be a place where we can give them leadership, provide some order, and establish harmony.

GRANVILLE SHARP: Apparently they lack discipline, Mr Clarkson.

JOHN CLARKSON: I am sure they will, in time, eventually discipline themselves.

GRANVILLE SHARP: (*To ELIZA.*) Will you be sailing with Mr Clarkson and assisting him in the establishment of this new venture?

ELIZA SHARP: We two alone? Dear Granville, must I once more remind you that there are no willing blacks, and I do not believe there is any urgent necessity for the establishment of a white colony in Africa, do you?

(*The English SERVANT enters and looks nervously at GRANVILLE SHARP, who eventually realizes that the SERVANT is standing there.*)

GRANVILLE SHARP: Yes, Daniel. What is it?

SERVANT: There is a man who is demanding an audience with you, sir.

GRANVILLE SHARP: 'Demanding'? At this hour of the night?

SERVANT: He appears to be somewhat agitated.

ELIZA SHARP: Then perhaps you should usher in my brother's impatient guest. (*The SERVANT withdraws.*) Are you expecting company, Granville?

GRANVILLE SHARP: No, of course not.

(*The English SERVANT reenters with THOMAS PETERS, who stands some way off.*)

THOMAS PETERS: Mr Granville Sharp?

GRANVILLE SHARP: That is correct.

THOMAS PETERS: My name is Thomas Peters. Your own name is well known to the black pioneers who recently served in the American war.

GRANVILLE SHARP: You are an American?

THOMAS PETERS: There are those who might style me thus. I gave service for the king during the recent exchange. Many of my complexion took up arms against the colonists in exchange for our freedom, and our passage to British soil. We served as spies for you, guides through swamps, pilots over treacherous sandbars, we dug trenches, buried bodies, drummed regiments in and out of danger, and our women cooked, laundered and nursed for you British.

GRANVILLE SHARP: Then you must come in, sir. Come closer.

(*THOMAS PETERS comes closer, but he still keeps his distance.*)

ELIZA SHARP: There is no need to be afraid.

THOMAS PETERS: I am not afraid.

GRANVILLE SHARP: Have you travelled here from America?

THOMAS PETERS: From a part of America called Nova Scotia. It is a wasteland to the north of known civilization. A cold, inhospitable place to which we have endured forced transportation.

GRANVILLE SHARP: And you now travel to London for what purpose, Mr Peters?

THOMAS PETERS: For justice for my people who fought honourably on the side of King George III with a promise of freedom, land and shelter upon the conclusion of hostilities. But we have been abandoned, and I fear our community will not survive another winter in this Nova Scotia.

GRANVILLE SHARP: And so you wish to come to England?

THOMAS PETERS: We have earned the right to expect a better fate than Nova Scotia. We have among us all the trades; chimney sweeps, blacksmiths, rope makers, shoe makers, millers, tanners, painters, millwrights, weavers, skinners, coachmen, pilots and navigators, but we have nowhere to practise our trades for the whites of Nova Scotia do not wish us to reside among them.

ELIZA SHARP: But perhaps England is not the perfumed land that you imagine it to be?

THOMAS PETERS: England is not Nova Scotia, that is all I know. England is not a place of depravity and hardship that exists on the edge of the known world.

GRANVILLE SHARP: My sister is merely pointing out that your people are not always well used in this country.

THOMAS PETERS: I cannot imagine a place on this earth where we would be more ill used than we are at present.

ELIZA SHARP: And Mr Peters, what would you have my brother do?

THOMAS PETERS: We have all served the king, and we have therefore earned the right to reside in a decent place under his protection. Do you recognize the right of our claim, or do you believe, like some Englishmen that I have already spoken with, that we black veterans, having gained our liberty, show ill grace by asking for the bounty of the government? (*Pause.*) Well, Mr Sharp, what do you intend to do to help us?

GRANVILLE SHARP: It is not clear to me what I can do.

JOHN CLARKSON: I have listened to you, Mr Peters, and I recognize the right of your claim. It is our responsibility to aid those who have helped and assisted us in our time of need.

ELIZA SHARP: Bravo, Lieutenant Clarkson!

GRANVILLE SHARP: But is there not some official body from whom you black loyalists might seek aid and assistance?

THOMAS PETERS: Every person, whether friend or foe, directed me to you, sir.

GRANVILLE SHARP: I see. (*Pause.*) Do you consider yourselves to be British or American?

THOMAS PETERS: British or American, it matters not what you call us, for the very trade which reduced us to homelessness, and this supplication, deemed that from this time on we would no longer be men who can be securely tied to your nations. We are men shackled to our race. Call us what you will; British, American, African, your love of slavery has already determined that henceforth we shall always be black.

GRANVILLE SHARP: I assure you sir, I am no lover of slavery.

THOMAS PETERS: Then I ask you again, what do you propose to do, Mr Sharp? I do not need your sympathy, I need your action. (*Turns to JOHN CLARKSON.*) And you, sir, what do you propose to do? At least you and your wife have recognized the legitimacy of our claim.

JOHN CLARKSON: My wife?

THOMAS PETERS: Your woman.

ELIZA SHARP: His friend. (*Pause.*) That only. His friend.

THOMAS PETERS: (*To JOHN CLARKSON.*) You appear to me to be a man of action. Are you able to press beyond mere words?

(*JOHN CLARKSON and THOMAS PETERS stare at each other. Neither man says another word.*)

INTERVAL

Act Two

SCENE TEN

We are in a meeting house in Nova Scotia where a congregation of black SETTLERS are gathered and singing a hymn. There are among them a few curious white NOVA SCOTIANS who stand at the back. The atmosphere is bleak, the hymn austere, and from the manner in which people clutch cloaks and wraps about them it is clearly winter. At the conclusion of the hymn a nervous-looking JOHN CLARKSON climbs to his feet and begins to address those gathered.

JOHN CLARKSON: Good day to you all. (*A few murmur 'Good day' in response.*) Some among you may already be aware that my name is John Clarkson and I was formerly engaged in His Majesty's service as a naval officer. This represents my first visit to Nova Scotia, and I am in command of a vessel which I hope to place at your disposal, but more of this in a moment. First, I wish to thank Mr Thomas Peters for bringing your plight to my attention. (*He gestures to THOMAS PETERS, who sits with SALLY. THOMAS PETERS appears to be slightly detached, physically and otherwise, from the other members of the congregation.*) Mr Peters recently made a courageous journey to London where he spoke with great force and passion about what he considered to be a betrayal of you people by we British.

ISAAC: My name is Isaac. Mr Peters spoke the truth. We were promised land grants and suitable soil, but instead we have been set down and left to rot.

JOHN CLARKSON: I was persuaded by much that Mr Peters conveyed, but you must not think of yourselves as having been abandoned.

ISAAC: We shall not tolerate a word against Mr Peters.

JOHN CLARKSON: I assure you, Isaac, that none who heard Mr Peters' pleas on your behalf in London could have anything but the highest regard for this man. (*He takes an envelope from his breast pocket, opens it, and retrieves a paper.*) I wish to read from an official edict prepared for you by the newly formed Sierra Leone Company.

ISAAC: Who are these people?

JOHN CLARKSON: (*Reads.*) 'The Sierra Leone Company offers free passage to Sierra Leone, and resettlement on fine and fertile land in Africa, for all who served His Majesty in the recent war. The Company expressly opposes the evil of slaving and exists only for the purpose of spreading moral well-being and propagating mutual wealth in a society in which members shall determine how, and by whom, they are to be governed.'

(*JOHN CLARKSON sets the paper to one side.*)

ISAAC: Who shall own the land on which we are to settle?

JOHN CLARKSON: Each individual will hold the freehold to their land and they will be free to participate in the commercial ventures of the Sierra Leone Company. There will be incentives for those who choose to work with the company, but every man is free to pursue his business according to his own pleasure providing he abides by the rules of the community.

ISAAC: And the rules are to be established by the whites?

JOHN CLARKSON: By the Sierra Leone Company, but subject to review by members who shall be elected from your numbers. (*Pause. The black SETTLERS begin to talk among themselves.*) The company's commercial agent is already in Sierra Leone preparing for our arrival.

FIRST WHITE NOVA SCOTIAN: We Nova Scotians have been living with these blacks since they arrived among us. Why should our blacks leave us and go to a land of great danger that is likely to prove injurious to their health and well-being?

JOHN CLARKSON: Mr Thomas Peters used similar words when describing this land. Nova Scotia, he stated, is a land that is proving injurious to our health and well-being.

I now understand the wisdom of his words. (*The black SETTLERS laugh.*)

SECOND WHITE NOVA SCOTIAN: But I believe the first settlement failed, is that not true? Is this an improved scheme?

JOHN CLARKSON: Do I detect on your part, sir, some wish for the Sierra Leone Company to fail? Is there some fear that you may well be losing your source of cheap labour?

(*There is a minor uproar among the WHITE NOVA SCOTIANS and the BLACK SETTLERS.*)

FIRST WHITE NOVA SCOTIAN: My only fear is for your sanity, sir. Coming here and proposing to transport Christian blacks to a heathen land. You cannot meddle with God's wishes.

DAVID GEORGE: (*Stands somewhat unsteadily.*) And is it God's wish that we should work for you until we drop dead of exhaustion in this bare and barren world? Do you believe that God wishes us to toil unceasingly for you?

JOHN CLARKSON: Mr Peters, do you have an opinion about God's wishes?

DAVID GEORGE: Mr Thomas Peters has no God, but let us not disrespect him for this. He has undertaken a voyage of much courage, and we owe him a debt of gratitude.

THOMAS PETERS: Thank you, David George, but I do not need your gratitude. I did what I knew to be right. I acted for all of you, and I shall continue to represent you to the best of my abilities. However, should you choose to follow a white Moses across the water, then I cannot argue with you.

DAVID GEORGE: Mr Peters, there is no competition here for leadership. Please, let us not create one.

JOHN CLARKSON: I am no white Moses, but I undertake to do my utmost on behalf of all of you. I shall never abandon you until each individual has assured me that he is perfectly satisfied that I should withdraw from your circle. My sole purpose is to be of service.

DAVID GEORGE: And your word is your bond?

JOHN CLARKSON: Before the Lord, I do solemnly swear that it is. Furthermore, in Africa blacks will be paid at the same rate as their white counterparts. I shall personally issue land certificates to each man and his family, and no rent is to be charged for use of the soil. In this utopia there will be self-government, and in return for your patience and good behaviour I will defend you with my life.

THOMAS PETERS: With your life, Mr Clarkson?

JOHN CLARKSON: With my life, Mr Peters. This new Freetown, which shall rise from the ashes of the Province of Freedom, will be the Jerusalem of Sierra Leone. A place where you shall be encouraged to throw off the shackles of slavery and behave like men.

DAVID GEORGE: Well I, for one, am happy to take you as our Governor. If we are to survive we shall need guidance from both heaven and earth. I entrust you, Mr Clarkson, to help us here on earth.

JOHN CLARKSON: Thank you, Mr George. (*Pause.*) Let us begin the registration of those who wish to sail.

(*DAVID GEORGE begins to marshal the CROWD. THOMAS and SALLY PETERS walk off.*)

DAVID GEORGE: Order! There is no need for this pushing.

FIRST SETTLER: I must go with Mr Clarkson!

DAVID GEORGE: There is room for everybody. Form a proper line. (*Points to MAN with his WIFE and CHILD.*) You may step forward. (*The FAMILY moves forward and stands before JOHN CLARKSON. To the others.*) You cannot take furniture with you. No tables or chairs. No beds. Pots and pans must be secured in sealed barrels.

SECOND SETTLER: What about our livestock?

DAVID GEORGE: Poultry, yes. But no pigs. And one of each animal that is permitted. So one dog only.

FIRST SETTLER: (*Laughs.*) Mr George, you are like Noah guarding the entrance to the ark.

DAVID GEORGE: As was the case with Noah, and those in his ark, we too must survive a period of difficulty before we once again make a safe landfall.

(*JOHN CLARKSON addresses the FAMILY.*)

JOHN CLARKSON: But only two of you will be sailing?

INDENTURED MAN: I am indentured for ten years to a man hereabouts. It was the only way to survive the winter.

JOHN CLARKSON: And so you will remain behind and work for this man for ten years, yet you wish to send your wife and child to Africa?

INDENTURED MAN: It breaks my heart to part from them. (*Pause.*) Even if you do sell them into slavery at least they will have escaped this Godless place.

JOHN CLARKSON: Sell them into slavery?

INDENTURED MAN: There is talk among some men that you plan to sell us.

JOHN CLARKSON: White men?

INDENTURED MAN: Yes sir.

JOHN CLARKSON: Is your master in the vicinity?

INDENTURED MAN: Over yonder, sir.

JOHN CLARKSON: (*To ATTENDANT.*) Bring the man before me. (*The ATTENDANT leaves.*) There will be no slavery. And I will not permit any distinction between black and white. Do you believe me?

INDENTURED MAN: For the sake of my wife and child, I hope so, sir.

(*The ATTENDANT brings the SLAVE OWNER before JOHN CLARKSON.*)

JOHN CLARKSON: Is it true, sir, that you would separate this man from his wife and child?

SLAVE OWNER: This man is bonded to work for me. He'll soon understand that he's better off with me.

JOHN CLARKSON: There will be no re-enslavement of these people.

SLAVE OWNER: They will all die of disease or malnutrition. (*Points.*) Either way, this one's better off with me.

JOHN CLARKSON: I wish to purchase this man's freedom from you.

SLAVE OWNER: You will leave us only the sick or the lazy. This man is too valuable for you to purchase.

JOHN CLARKSON: Is your heart made of stone? Can you not see the tears in the man's eyes?

SLAVE OWNER: In a strong wind my eyes also brim with water.

JOHN CLARKSON: (*To ATTENDANT.*) Have David George issue certificates of passage for the wife and child. (*The ATTENDANT leaves. To SLAVE OWNER.*) I have to attend to another matter.

SLAVE OWNER: You are content to allow me to keep my own property?

JOHN CLARKSON: This is a man, sir. This is not property. A horse or a goat is your property, but not your fellow man.

(*JOHN CLARKSON exits. Lights up on THOMAS and SALLY PETERS sitting in their rudimentary house. THOMAS looks at her.*)

THOMAS PETERS: You should be resting.

SALLY PETERS: But I am not tired.

THOMAS PETERS: You must rest for the sake of our child. Clara is gone but we have the chance of another child. I do not want anything to go wrong.

SALLY PETERS: Thomas, you have been quiet. What are you thinking?

THOMAS PETERS: You know better than to ask me this.

SALLY PETERS: We must leave this Nova Scotia or we shall perish. (*Pause.*) Please, Thomas. I do not wish to lose another child to this place.

(*There is a knock on the door. THOMAS PETERS stands.*)

THOMAS PETERS: Sally, I have no desire to follow another white man, but I am not foolish. I understand that we cannot stay here.

(*He moves off and returns with JOHN CLARKSON, who removes his hat as he enters. He bows slightly towards SALLY PETERS.*)

JOHN CLARKSON: Mrs Peters

SALLY PETERS: Good day, Mr Clarkson.

JOHN CLARKSON: I am sorry to disturb your peace but I need to speak with your husband.

THOMAS PETERS: Whatever you have to say to me you can also say to my wife.

SALLY PETERS: (*Begins to stand.*) No, I will leave you men…

THOMAS PETERS: Sit down, Sally. (*To JOHN CLARKSON.*) Have you come to once more proclaim your good intentions?

JOHN CLARKSON: Not exactly.

THOMAS PETERS: Then what? You appear disturbed, Mr Clarkson.

JOHN CLARKSON: Mr Peters, I have come to remind you that on board ship there can be but one captain. And I am that man. And as it is upon the sea, so shall it be on land.

THOMAS PETERS: (*Laughs.*) Your humour surprises me. If this is all you have to say, then I bid you a good day, Mr Clarkson.

JOHN CLARKSON: You would do well to heed my words.

THOMAS PETERS: You threaten me?

JOHN CLARKSON: I tell you the truth.

(*THOMAS PETERS moves closer to JOHN CLARKSON.*)

SALLY PETERS: Please, Thomas. The man means to cause no offence.

JOHN CLARKSON: Truly, I seek only to clarify our situation, for the sake of all concerned.

THOMAS PETERS: If you betray these men, I will kill you.

JOHN CLARKSON: Your words and your manner are unnecessarily offensive.

THOMAS PETERS: You can lead us to Africa, but once we arrive on land I will take charge of affairs.

JOHN CLARKSON: Now it is you who dares to threaten me.

THOMAS PETERS: I speak my mind, and I do so without fear. (*Moves closer.*) Listen closely. I will *kill* you if you betray us.

JOHN CLARKSON: Then you give me little choice but to leave you behind in Nova Scotia.

SALLY PETERS: No!

JOHN CLARKSON: For our new community to survive we must have harmony.

THOMAS PETERS: (*To SALLY PETERS.*) This man would not dare to travel to Africa and leave me behind. Do not worry. He has not the courage to act on his words. (*Pause.*) But I will act on mine. And Mr Clarkson understands this.

(*THOMAS PETERS and JOHN CLARKSON stare at each other.*)

SCENE ELEVEN

We are at sea. In the darkness we can hear a violent storm that is raging and the ship is being tempest-tossed first one way and then the other. Lightning is flashing and thunder roaring. As the lights come up we see a seriously ailing JOHN CLARKSON lying in bed attended to by DAVID and PHYLLIS GEORGE. It is clear that JOHN CLARKSON is near death and his feverish brain is racing.

DAVID GEORGE: (*To PHYLLIS.*) More boiling water, and please send Isaac in with fresh towels. (*PHYLLIS hesitates for a moment as she looks at JOHN CLARKSON.*) Well, what are you waiting for? Phyllis, this is not the time for contemplation. Mr Clarkson is ailing.

(*PHYLLIS GEORGE dashes from the room and DAVID GEORGE turns his attention back to JOHN CLARKSON, who takes DAVID GEORGE's hand.*)

JOHN CLARKSON: I am sorry. Perhaps you will tell Eliza.

DAVID GEORGE: Eliza? I am afraid I know of no Eliza.

JOHN CLARKSON: Come, come, my good fellow, surely you know Eliza. The sister of Mr Granville Sharp. She is a most headstrong woman.

(*JOHN CLARKSON sits up slightly as he 'sees' ELIZA SHARP appear before him. ELIZA SHARP smiles at him.*)

(*To ELIZA SHARP.*) Was there something defective in my person that led you away from me?

DAVID GEORGE: I am sorry, Mr Clarkson. I do not understand.

JOHN CLARKSON: I am speaking with Eliza. (*Points.*) She remains as beautiful as ever. (*Pause. Irritated.*) Do you not see her?

DAVID GEORGE: I cannot see her.

JOHN CLARKSON: (*Points.*) There, man! There!

DAVID GEORGE: I am sorry, Mr Clarkson.

JOHN CLARKSON: My life appears to be constructed so as to deprive me of the luxury of affections. (*ELIZA SHARP begins to walk off.*) No! Please, do not leave me, Eliza. Stay a while, dear lady.

DAVID GEORGE: One must minister to the heart as well as the mind.

JOHN CLARKSON: I am led to believe that love is a most powerful emotion.

DAVID GEORGE: It is God's gift to us, Mr Clarkson. It nourishes our souls.

JOHN CLARKSON: And now Eliza is gone. She is no more.

DAVID GEORGE: She is with you in spirit.

JOHN CLARKSON: I wish this vessel to in no way resemble a slaving ship. The decks must be swept three times a day.

DAVID GEORGE: Sorry, sir?

JOHN CLARKSON: This must be a floating republic of Christian harmony, do you understand me?

DAVID GEORGE: You must rest, Mr Clarkson. There is no need to disturb your mind with troubling thoughts. You have given great service.

JOHN CLARKSON: We have a responsibility to assist you people and help you seize your own destiny.

DAVID GEORGE: Rest, Mr Clarkson. You mind is full of fever.

JOHN CLARKSON: On this ship you must think of yourself as a passenger en route to Africa. Every last member of the crew must treat you with respect or they shall be punished.

(*ISAAC enters with an armful of clean towels. He struggles to keep his balance as the ship tosses this way and that.*)

DAVID GEORGE: Set them down, Isaac, and then go and help my wife with the fresh water.

ISAAC: Yes, Mr George.

DAVID GEORGE: How many times must I tell you? I am David, your minister. When the fearful storms came you asked me to baptize you and now, in the eyes of the Lord, we are both his children. There can be no distinction.

ISAAC: I understand.

DAVID GEORGE: Isaac, please try and find my wife as soon as possible. We need water. (*ISAAC leaves the cabin. DAVID GEORGE picks up a towel and begins to mop JOHN CLARKSON's brow.*)

JOHN CLARKSON: (*Coughs.*) My brother, Thomas. The abolitionist. Perhaps you have heard his name?

DAVID GEORGE: Of course, every man knows of Thomas Clarkson. (*Pause.*) Should an accident befall you, do you have a message for him?

JOHN CLARKSON: I hope I have not disappointed him. This was always my greatest fear. But now, to fail to reach Africa. (*Pause.*) I have sullied my brother's name.

DAVID GEORGE: You have done no such thing. Over one thousand men have willingly followed you into the heart of this raging ocean. Men who trust you to deliver them to Africa and freedom.

JOHN CLARKSON: Then how foolish of me to abandon you here, our journey still in peril and incomplete.

(*PHYLLIS GEORGE and ISAAC appear with water. DAVID GEORGE turns to them.*)

DAVID GEORGE: We must quell the fever. Quickly, soak the towels, and then wring out the excess water.

JOHN CLARKSON: (*Gestures impatiently.*) Foolish, foolish. (*DAVID GEORGE takes his hand.*) It is no use, Mr George. Now you must lead the men to Sierra Leone. Please tender my apologies to the company agent, Mr Falconbridge. He will welcome you to the African utopia.

DAVID GEORGE: Please, no more talk. Preserve your strength.

(*PHYLLIS and ISAAC bring the towels and begin to apply them to JOHN CLARKSON.*)

JOHN CLARKSON: Mr George, this fever is too much to bear.

(*JOHN CLARKSON releases DAVID GEORGE's hand. CLARKSON's eyes fall shut, and PHYLLIS GEORGE begins to weep. DAVID GEORGE gets up and goes to her and comforts her in his arms.*)

DAVID GEORGE: I am afraid he has passed to the next world. (*To ISAAC.*) Summon the men, Isaac.

(ISAAC leaves and bells begin to toll. Six MEN enter and drape a Union Jack over the body of JOHN CLARKSON. They then lift JOHN CLARKSON into a rudimentary open-ended coffin, which they hoist onto their shoulders. They slow-march up to the deck level. DAVID and PHYLLIS GEORGE follow until they reach the deck. THOMAS PETERS stands by himself and watches the MEN set down the coffin. All the MEN and CREW are gathered on deck as the bell continues to toll. THOMAS PETERS addresses them.)

THOMAS PETERS: And so Mr Clarkson could lead us only this far and no further. But we must not criticize him for he gave us good service. And he did so with courage. When I journeyed to London there were many who would listen, but there were few who were prepared to act. Therefore, as we cast his body to the deep we should acknowledge this. I have no words of Christianity to offer. I will leave this to David George who, as you all know, appears to be guided in his actions by the book known as the Bible.

DAVID GEORGE: You speak as though this is something I ought to be ashamed of? But I am proud to follow my God, the father of all mankind. And, at a time like this, I beg for his guidance as I seek to lead us all safely to Africa.

THOMAS PETERS: *You* seek to lead us?

DAVID GEORGE: It was Mr Clarkson's dying wish that I should assume command.

THOMAS PETERS: Can any others claim to have heard this instruction?

DAVID GEORGE: Do you imagine that I would speak falsehoods to you?

THOMAS PETERS: Mr George, do you forget that I have seen you on the field of battle. You are no leader.

DAVID GEORGE: I shall try my best.

THOMAS PETERS: *(Laughs. He points to the six MEN.)* You men, the coffin. *(The six MEN hoist the coffin onto their shoulders. As they do so PHYLLIS GEORGE points.)*

PHYLLIS GEORGE: Mr Clarkson stirred.

DAVID GEORGE: Set down the body!

THOMAS PETERS: No! (*The six MEN holding the coffin hover, not quite knowing what to do.*) This is no time for superstition and Christian magic. We must be dignified.

DAVID GEORGE: And you would condemn a man to be tossed alive into the ocean? This is not dignified, it is barbarous.

THOMAS PETERS: (*To PHYLLIS GEORGE.*) Are you certain he is alive?

(*DAVID GEORGE crosses to the coffin, which the men lower. He puts his hand against CLARKSON's heart.*)

DAVID GEORGE: My wife is not mistaken. There is the slightest murmur. (*To the MEN bearing the coffin.*) Downstairs to his quarters. (*To PHYLLIS and ISAAC.*) Go with Mr Clarkson and make sure that he is comforted.

(*There is much activity as the six MEN bear the coffin back in the direction of CLARKSON's cabin. PHYLLIS and ISAAC move off with the coffin. We can see the coffin's arrival in the cabin and PHYLLIS and ISAAC begin to attend to JOHN CLARKSON. On deck DAVID GEORGE and THOMAS PETERS face each other.*)

Do you have any respect for me?

THOMAS PETERS: It will be for the people to decide who shall lead them, and not for the white man to appoint somebody that he feels he can trust.

DAVID GEORGE: Can he not trust you?

THOMAS PETERS: I do not trust any white man. For them 'freedom' is a principle. For us it is a matter of life and death. This being the case I cannot allow such men to have control of my life. I will talk with them as an equal, but I shall never be ruled by them.

(*We see JOHN CLARKSON begin to rise a little from the bed. PHYLLIS GEORGE gives him some water. ISAAC moves to leave the cabin.*)

DAVID GEORGE: Tell me, Thomas Peters, what do you truly want?

THOMAS PETERS: I wish to live freely as a man.

DAVID GEORGE: Beyond any rules or discipline? Beyond any organization?

THOMAS PETERS: Beyond the white man's rules.

DAVID GEORGE: And the black man's rules, will they be more humane? Will they embrace liberty and respect freedom? Is this what we can look forward to in your world?

THOMAS PETERS: In my Africa the white man will either treat us with respect or know his place.

DAVID GEORGE: In *your* Africa?

THOMAS PETERS: Yes, we are sailing to *my* Africa. Africa is nothing to do with the white man. It is *my* Africa! Your Africa, if you so wish!

(*ISAAC approaches the two men.*)

ISAAC: Excuse me, but Mr Clarkson is conscious. (*To DAVID GEORGE.*) Your wife proclaims it a miracle. The fever has broken and Mr Clarkson may yet achieve a full recovery.

DAVID GEORGE: Gather the men on deck.

ISAAC: Yes, Mr George.

(*ISAAC moves off. We see the MEN and CREW beginning to assemble.*)

THOMAS PETERS: 'Yes, Mr George'?

DAVID GEORGE: I have asked him on many occasions to address me as David, but it appears that he has fallen into the practice.

THOMAS PETERS: Indeed he has…Mr George.

DAVID GEORGE: Thomas, if we cannot be civil with one another at least let us embrace peace. For the sake of the enterprise. (*Pause. THOMAS PETERS stares at DAVID GEORGE.*) Well?

THOMAS PETERS: I know you, David George. (*Pause.*) I am watching you.

(The MEN are now gathered all about. ISAAC appears back on deck.)

ISAAC: *(To DAVID GEORGE.)* I am afraid many men are sick.

DAVID GEORGE: Thank you, Isaac. This number is enough. *(To the MEN.)* It appears that Mr Clarkson may well survive and complete this blessed journey with us. Let us raise our voices in thanks and prepare ourselves for the new country.

(Their voices are raised in a melodious hymn of praise.)

MEN: Awake! And sing the song, of Moses and the Lamb
Awake! Every heart and every tongue
To praise the Saviour's name!
The day of Jubilee is come
Return ye ransomed sinners home...

(As the hymn is being sung JOHN CLARKSON climbs from his bed and begins to put on his uniform. He then moves to the bow of the ship where he stares out at land. The sun begins to rise as the hymn fades out. ISAAC disturbs his reverie.)

ISAAC: Mr Clarkson.

JOHN CLARKSON: Yes, Isaac. Is it not a joyous wonder to once more gaze out upon land?

ISAAC: We are all grateful to you for conducting us safely to Africa.

JOHN CLARKSON: Do not thank me, Isaac. You must thank God who is the master of us all. Do you have faith?

ISAAC: I have been baptized. By Mr George.

JOHN CLARKSON: Indeed he is a leader of men.

ISAAC: He is a preacher.

JOHN CLARKSON: And you are his flock. *(ISAAC looks closely at JOHN CLARKSON but says nothing.)*

ISAAC: A launch has reached our ship, and your visitors request an audience with you.

JOHN CLARKSON: My visitors?

ISAAC: The company agent, Mr Alexander Falconbridge, and his wife.

JOHN CLARKSON: Well usher them into my presence, Isaac. No time to lose.

(*ISAAC disappears for a moment and then leads ALEXANDER FALCONBRIDGE and ANNA MARIA towards JOHN CLARKSON. FALCONBRIDGE looks a little unsteady on his feet, as though he has been drinking.*)

FALCONBRIDGE: Well, after two months in this hot and humid place, I am finally able to welcome you to our African world. Might I present my wife, Anna Maria.

ANNA MARIA: An honour, Mr Clarkson. Your courage and determination are widely known and spoken of.

JOHN CLARKSON: You surely exaggerate, Mrs Falconbridge. I am simply grateful to have completed this difficult journey in some health. I am also happy to be able to discharge courteous and able passengers who are keen to commence a new life.

FALCONBRIDGE: (*Points.*) Our somewhat rudimentary town, Freetown, lies before us. The land is established as ours, but we must still be aware of local hostility.

JOHN CLARKSON: But has the company not solved this problem of the ownership of land? These passengers all hold certificates entitling them to freehold parcels of this soil.

FALCONBRIDGE: We have solved the problem, to some extent. But these Africans are unpredictable. They neither possess our intelligence nor our sensibility.

ANNA MARIA: Please, Alexander. You know such sentiments help nobody.

FALCONBRIDGE: For God's sake, woman. Be quiet!

ANNA MARIA: I shall be quiet when you have learned how to curb your tongue.

(*There is momentary silence as JOHN CLARKSON is shocked by the severity of the FALCONBRIDGES' exchange.*)

FALCONBRIDGE: (*To JOHN CLARKSON.*) We need more time to negotiate with these people for this land. But where are the necessary supplies to construct the public buildings?

JOHN CLARKSON: Have the company not dispatched materials and men?

FALCONBRIDGE: Those few white men who sailed with me are now run wild. Semi-white savages.

ANNA MARIA: They are either diseased or frightened.

FALCONBRIDGE: These useless men were never meant to labour. We require fresh supplies!

JOHN CLARKSON: The company have sent nothing?

FALCONBRIDGE: We have our shelters, but the blacks must find some scrap of land and build their own.

JOHN CLARKSON: But promises have been made to these subjects of the king.

FALCONBRIDGE: The blacks?

JOHN CLARKSON: They are the king's subjects.

ANNA MARIA: Are they prepared to labour, or do they merely wish to besport themselves as residents?

FALCONBRIDGE: One cannot make fine wine from brackish water. Speaking of which, a drink Mr Clarkson? To your good health. (*Points to ISAAC.*) Can you not send the boy?

JOHN CLARKSON: The man's name is Isaac.

FALCONBRIDGE: Isaac, be a good fellow and track down some port.

ANNA MARIA: Alexander, please.

JOHN CLARKSON: (*To ISAAC.*) By all means, Isaac. Port and three glasses.

FALCONBRIDGE: Two is all that will be necessary. My wife frowns upon such indulgence.

JOHN CLARKSON: Two glasses please, Isaac.

FALCONBRIDGE: And don't delay, my good fellow. (*ISAAC leaves. To JOHN CLARKSON.*) Are your blacks ready for a challenge?

JOHN CLARKSON: They are not 'my blacks'.

FALCONBRIDGE: (*Laughs.*) Until this voyage you have never had command of any but white men, am I right? (*JOHN CLARKSON says nothing in return.*) I thought so. They need guidance, Mr Clarkson. A white 'father' figure. We must prepare ourselves for a long battle if we wish to keep good order in this place. (*ISAAC returns with two glasses of port on a tray. FALCONBRIDGE grabs his.*) A toast. To Africa. Few come out, though many go in. (*FALCONBRIDGE raises his glass and drinks. JOHN CLARKSON reluctantly joins him.*) This evening I shall introduce you to the council. (*JOHN CLARKSON looks puzzled.*) The men from London who are here to run the colony. Under your leadership, of course.

JOHN CLARKSON: The semi-white savages?

FALCONBRIDGE: (*Laughs.*) Perhaps I exaggerate a little.

JOHN CLARKSON: The colony shall be run by a freely elected assembly of settlers.

FALCONBRIDGE: Yes, white settlers, Mr Clarkson.

JOHN CLARKSON: We shall work together, black and white.

FALCONBRIDGE: (*Laughs.*) I think not!

ANNA MARIA: My husband is of the opinion that there exists a great and permanent distinction between black and white. (*To FALCONBRIDGE.*) I fear, Alexander, that Mr Clarkson does not subscribe to your beliefs.

JOHN CLARKSON: Black and white together. These are the principles of the Sierra Leone Company.

FALCONBRIDGE: Well, sir, it would appear that the company have somewhat modified their original principles. Black council members are certainly not part of the order of things in our world.

JOHN CLARKSON: (*To ISAAC.*) Perhaps you might leave us for a moment, Isaac.

ISAAC: Yes, of course.

ANNA MARIA: (*To ISAAC.*) My husband means no disrespect.

(*ISAAC pauses for a moment then moves away.*)

JOHN CLARKSON: (*To FALCONBRIDGE.*) Are you drunk, sir?

FALCONBRIDGE: Drunk?

JOHN CLARKSON: Answer me directly.

FALCONBRIDGE: (*Laughs.*) Drunk? I am happy, sir. Happy to see you.

ANNA MARIA: During these past two months we have suffered much hardship and, quite frankly, our councillors are hardly men of the first rank. Discipline, Lieutenant Clarkson, is not their strong suit.

JOHN CLARKSON: Then perhaps my black passengers might offer them some lessons in this area. Mr Falconbridge, tomorrow morning assemble these so-called white councilmen together for I wish to address them.

FALCONBRIDGE: To what purpose?

JOHN CLARKSON: I beg your pardon.

ANNA MARIA: I shall endeavor to remind my husband of your request. His mind is apt to wander.

JOHN CLARKSON: Madam, this is not a request, it is an order. (*Signals to ISAAC.*) Isaac, come please. (*ISAAC moves forward.*) Prepare the passengers for arrival at Freetown. We have much to do before sunset. (*ISAAC moves off. The FALCONBRIDGES still wait.*) Is there something further?

FALCONBRIDGE: We are dismissed?

JOHN CLARKSON: Take care of your health, sir. A man of your years and experience might yet prove extremely valuable in the task that lies ahead of us.

(*ANNA MARIA moves to take FALCONBRIDGE's arm, but he shakes her off.*)

SCENE TWELVE

THOMAS PETERS is chopping wood with an axe. He is stripped to the waist and clearly he has been labouring hard. SALLY PETERS sits propped up on a chair and wrapped in a blanket. She seems feverish.

THOMAS PETERS: Sally, do you need more water? (*She shakes her head.*) I can fix you some food?

SALLY PETERS: Finish your work, Thomas. They say the rainy season will soon come.

THOMAS PETERS: But not before I finish building this cabin. No rain is going to fall on my wife's head.

SALLY PETERS: I'm sorry, Thomas.

THOMAS PETERS: You have no reason to be sorry, Sally. Not now, not ever.

SALLY PETERS: My body just isn't strong enough to bear any more children. I've let you down, Thomas. And now, I don't seem to be able to unburden myself from this fever.

THOMAS PETERS: Woman, how many times do you want me to tell you? I married you because I loved you. I don't need a breeding woman. I need a loving woman, and I have the finest in you. You wrap up tight and we shall burn that fever right out of your body.

SALLY PETERS: I'm frightened, Thomas.

THOMAS PETERS: I've already told you a dozen times, Sally. Some people can afford fears and some people cannot afford to be fooling with such emotions. We are not a fearing people, Sally.

SALLY PETERS: I'm cold.

THOMAS PETERS: You want me to hold you? (*He puts down his axe and moves to her and hugs her close.*) This making you feel better? (*SALLY PETERS nods.*) We are home now, woman. (*He gestures.*) This soil beneath our feet, this sky above our heads, we own everything here. It belongs to us. We are home.

SALLY PETERS: Thomas, you said we should live apart from the others, and although I had no desire to do so I said yes. But, Thomas, every day you insist on going and speaking to our people, and all the while you are stirring up their blood. What are you planning? Tell me, I am your wife.

(*THOMAS PETERS moves away from her. He stands a pace or two away and looks at her.*)

THOMAS PETERS: Do you want a husband who ignores injustice?

SALLY PETERS: Thomas, why do you have to fight every battle in every war? Can we not just form an island of two in this Africa? I am tired.

THOMAS PETERS: Then dear wife you must rest, but I have my work.

SALLY PETERS: Are you going to kill Mr Clarkson?

THOMAS PETERS: He has broken his promises to us.

SALLY PETERS: You have not answered my question.

THOMAS PETERS: I have given him a chance to keep his promises.

SALLY PETERS: You are plotting to kill him, aren't you?

THOMAS PETERS: Woman, stop bothering me.

SALLY PETERS: Tell me truly, am I a burden to you? (*THOMAS PETERS says nothing.*) I suppose I have my answer.

THOMAS PETERS: You are not a burden, Sally. But your words trouble me. I need you to support me.

SALLY PETERS: I do support you! You are my husband, and I want what is good for you. But Thomas, I am not sure how much more help I can offer to you if you continue to look for trouble. I tell you, I am tired.

THOMAS PETERS: Rest, Sally, and you will be strong again. I am sure of it.

(*JOHN CLARKSON, ALEXANDER FALCONBRIDGE, ANNA MARIA FALCONBRIDGE and two white council members, MR*

GREEN and MR WILSON, wearing council sashes, approach THOMAS PETERS.)

JOHN CLARKSON: Mr Peters, forgive our unannounced intrusion. (*To SALLY PETERS.*) Mrs Peters.

THOMAS PETERS: Mr Clarkson.

SALLY PETERS: (*Stands.*) Forgive me. I must lie in the shade.

JOHN CLARKSON: I hope we have not driven you away.

THOMAS PETERS: My wife makes her own decisions. (*To SALLY.*) Shall I bring you another blanket?

SALLY PETERS: (*Shakes her head. To the visitors.*) You must excuse me. (*SALLY PETERS moves off.*)

JOHN CLARKSON: (*To THOMAS PETERS.*) I believe you know Mr and Mrs Falconbridge. Mr Wilson and Mr Green are council members who know of your journey to England on behalf of your people.

(*MR WILSON and MR GREEN come forward and shake hands with a reluctant THOMAS PETERS.*)

MR GREEN / MR WILSON: A pleasure to meet you, Mr Peters.

JOHN CLARKSON: I see you still choose to live apart from us.

THOMAS PETERS: 'Us'?

JOHN CLARKSON: We are trying to build a community.

THOMAS PETERS: Blacks live with blacks and whites live with whites. There is no 'us'.

MR GREEN: (*To THOMAS PETERS.*) We cannot compel men to act against the prejudices in their heart.

JOHN CLARKSON: I wish that we all lived together, but these things take time. It is regretful.

THOMAS PETERS: (*To JOHN CLARKSON.*) And is this the feeling of all the whites?

JOHN CLARKSON: I speak only for myself.

THOMAS PETERS: I thought so.

FALCONBRIDGE: There is a natural order to all things, Mr Peters. Even here in Africa.

THOMAS PETERS: You do not belong in Africa, Mr Falconbridge.

FALCONBRIDGE: How about Mr Green or Mr Wilson. Do they belong here? Or Mr Clarkson. Is he too an unwelcome presence?

THOMAS PETERS: We have been lied to.

FALCONBRIDGE: I beg your pardon?

MR WILSON: Mr Peters, in our society to accuse a man of deliberately spreading falsehoods is a most serious charge.

THOMAS PETERS: (*Waves his hand dismissively.*) You people may go about your business and leave my wife and myself in peace. (*To FALCONBRIDGE.*) Take your woman and go.

ANNA MARIA: The impudence of this man!

JOHN CLARKSON: Mr Peters, we came to ask if you might consider joining the council.

THOMAS PETERS: The white man's council?

JOHN CLARKSON: Well it would no longer be the white man's council were you to sit with us.

FALCONBRIDGE: (*To JOHN CLARKSON.*) Are you sure that this is the correct way to proceed?

JOHN CLARKSON: Mr Falconbridge, we have discussed this matter and decided upon a course of action.

ANNA MARIA: (*Puts her hand on her husband's arm.*) Alexander, please do not excite yourself. The matter has already been settled.

FALCONBRIDGE: (*Snaps back at her.*) You take the side of this man and his blacks? Has the sun affected your mind?

ANNA MARIA: No, but I sometimes feel that drink has robbed you of your reason.

JOHN CLARKSON: (*To THOMAS PETERS.*) Perhaps yourself and David George can represent the views of your people.

THOMAS PETERS: David George? I take it that we two are acceptable to you?

FALCONBRIDGE: Not to me.

JOHN CLARKSON: (*To THOMAS PETERS.*) You appear to be the senior men.

(*THOMAS PETERS begins to laugh.*)

FALCONBRIDGE: (*To JOHN CLARKSON.*) Look, he mocks you. He openly makes sport.

THOMAS PETERS: You men consider me to be senior and worthy of responsibility?

JOHN CLARKSON: The offer is in earnest. Do we amuse you?

THOMAS PETERS: Away with you, Clarkson! Away with all of you! You have no right to determine who shall represent black men. We shall determine this for ourselves.

ANNA MARIA: (*To THOMAS PETERS.*) We have just paid you a great compliment.

THOMAS PETERS: Am I supposed to be grateful?

FALCONBRIDGE: Yes! Gratitude and modesty, these are virtues in a civilized world. (*To JOHN CLARKSON, ANNA MARIA, and MR GREEN and MR WILSON.*) Let us go. This pantomime has run its course.

JOHN CLARKSON: (*To THOMAS PETERS.*) But if your people were able to vote, you would both be elected. Surely we save time and effort by simply appointing you.

THOMAS PETERS: Mr Clarkson, I do not recognize your authority. Here in Africa, you have no status. Now leave my land!

(*The COUNCIL MEMBERS begin to move off, including the FALCONBRIDGES. JOHN CLARKSON remains behind. As they move off, ISAAC comes into view, leading an OLD BLIND MAN.*)

JOHN CLARKSON: Mr Peters, it *is* possible to combine strength of mind with civility. Perhaps nobody has pointed this out to you.

THOMAS PETERS: I have nothing further to say. You must take your begging to David George. Perhaps he will receive you with more gratitude. (*To ISAAC.*) Isaac, come, bring your father to sit. (*To JOHN CLARKSON.*) At least we have one happy story in the midst of this hypocrisy and cowardice. Isaac is reunited with the father he has not seen for many years.

JOHN CLARKSON: That is wonderful news.

THOMAS PETERS: Although his father can no longer see, he knows that Isaac has come home. To a land where he is free. Am I making myself clear, Mr Clarkson? Even a blind man knows that by setting foot on this land a black man is free and beyond your jurisdiction.

JOHN CLARKSON: There seems to be little purpose to conducting our discussion in an atmosphere of such hostility. I regret that you feel this way. (*Pause.*) I bid you good day, Mr Peters. Isaac.

(*ISAAC looks at JOHN CLARKSON, but he says nothing. After an awkward pause, JOHN CLARKSON leaves.*)

THOMAS PETERS: (*To ISAAC.*) Is your father well?

ISAAC: He is well, but I have forgotten so much of our native tongue. It is difficult to speak with him.

THOMAS PETERS: This slavery business has damaged our families, but everything will be fine.

ISAAC: After so many years in America this place no longer feels like home.

THOMAS PETERS: Give it time, Isaac. Like seeds in the wind we have been scattered. It will take time for us to once again root in Africa.

ISAAC: I love and honour my father, but he is a stranger to me now.

THOMAS PETERS: Your presence is comfort enough for him.

ISAAC: Did these men come to disturb you?

THOMAS PETERS: Do not worry yourself with these men, Isaac. We shall soon take care of them. (*Pause.*) Are you with me, Isaac?

ISAAC: I have followed you to Africa.

THOMAS PETERS: Followed me, or have you followed the white captain? There is a difference.

ISAAC: I have followed you, Mr Peters. Most of us have followed you to this place. I am sure Mr Clarkson knows this.

THOMAS PETERS: As long as Mr Clarkson dominates us there shall never be any peace.

ISAAC: He is not a bad man.

THOMAS PETERS: The point is he is the wrong man. A republic of black and white? Here, in Africa? He is a dangerous man.

(*ISAAC stares at THOMAS PETERS.*)

SCENE THIRTEEN

In the darkness a spotlight picks out THOMAS PETERS, who speaks directly to the audience.

THOMAS PETERS: In Nova Scotia we once again decided to cross the water, and clutching our papers of freedom and our land grants we arrived in this place that you call Freetown where you promised us that you would never again determine our fate for we would be at liberty to elect our own leaders. But there is no self-rule in this place. For over a year now we have endured the spectacle of this council of white men drinking the supplies, and eating the food in the stores. When we appeal to you, our so-called governor, to intervene on our behalf and demand that these drunken, diseased men who openly sneer at us be either disciplined or expelled from this community, you say that you are waiting to receive instruction from your company, but may I remind you that we did not follow your company to Africa. My people did not place their faith in the Sierra Leone Company, they placed their faith in a man who said that he would defend our rights with his life, but after a year you claim that you are still waiting to hear from your company, and after a year you continue to ask us to be patient and wait for the right to represent and govern ourselves.

(*As the lights come up we see DAVID GEORGE – who wears a company sash – PHYLLIS GEORGE, ALEXANDER and ANNA MARIA FALCONBRIDGE, ISAAC, and a group of SETTLERS. JOHN CLARKSON is among them and it is clear that THOMAS PETERS has been addressing JOHN CLARKSON. JOHN CLARKSON now steps forward.*)

JOHN CLARKSON: Mr Peters, I understand your frustration.

THOMAS PETERS: Do you? Do you understand the indignity you have visited on us all, Mr Clarkson?

JOHN CLARKSON: Utopia cannot be established in a week, or a month, or even a year. Might I hear another opinion?

THOMAS PETERS: (*Brandishes a piece of paper.*) I have more to say.

JOHN CLARKSON: Of course, Mr Peters. You may continue. I am sorry to hear of the recent loss of your wife Sally, but I am sure that she is safe in God's hands.

THOMAS PETERS: The matter I wish to address has no relevance to my wife or to your God. I have in my hand a list of my people's grievances. (*He hands the list to JOHN CLARKSON who takes it.*) Read it, Mr Clarkson. Read it instead of reading your Bible.

DAVID GEORGE: Mr Clarkson can read both the list and the Bible. The study of one does not negate his interest in the other.

THOMAS PETERS: (*To DAVID GEORGE.*) I have asked for a moment to address those gathered here. You will, I am sure, have your own opportunity.

DAVID GEORGE: Then continue, but I ask you to do so without insulting the beliefs of many gathered hereabouts.

THOMAS PETERS: Your superstitions are your own affair, I am only interested in stating the facts. We were promised ownership of our own land. We were promised self-government. We have neither. (*He turns directly to the SETTLERS.*) Who among you elected Mr Clarkson to be our representative? Was not the understanding that upon arrival we would assume control of our own fate? Who among you gave him permission to be our master here in Africa?

JOHN CLARKSON: I am not your master!

THOMAS PETERS: Do you not, together with the drunken Mr Falconbridge, make decisions on our behalf without consultation? Do not yourself and this red-faced man report back to London without any consideration for our wishes?

ANNA MARIA: My husband languishes with a fever, or he would speak for himself. But given his absence, I ask you to please, keep a civil tongue in your head when discussing Mr Falconbridge.

THOMAS PETERS: Madam, I have yet to hear him utter one civil word to you in public. Perhaps lessons in civility should begin closer to home.

ISAAC: Thomas, please. Let us focus on the matters at hand.

THOMAS PETERS: I might say the same to you too, Isaac. Do not be distracted by temptation.

ANNA MARIA: And just what do you mean by that?

DAVID GEORGE: Thomas, please.

JOHN CLARKSON: (*To THOMAS PETERS.*) Do you have a point that you wish to make, or are you simply determined that this pleasant morning should descend into acrimony?

THOMAS PETERS: We have no representation in this place, and your favourite, Mr David George, appears intent that it should remain the case for this enables him to personally seek your favours.

DAVID GEORGE: Until now, Thomas, we have managed to be of different minds yet maintain relations of some cordiality. But you now appear to be set upon destroying what little harmony remains between us by making personal attacks upon my character. Clearly we cannot work together so our people must make a choice.

THOMAS PETERS: (*Laughs.*) A choice? They have already presented their feelings to me. Mr Clarkson holds the evidence.

DAVID GEORGE: The evidence? Complaints bullied from men who were either too timid or too confused to stand against you.

JOHN CLARKSON: Mr George, that is enough. There is no need to press this dispute any further. Remember, I have appointed you a councilman. You do not need to stoop to this level. (*To THOMAS PETERS.*) Mr Peters, I have here a letter signed by a good number of settlers, whose names I have promised never to reveal, warning me of your intent to do damage to my person and replace me as governor of the Sierra Leone Colony. At first, I was sceptical of the letter, preferring to believe that any such talk on your part might well have been born of grief at having recently lost your wife. But now, as I listen to you, I wonder. Mr Peters, do you wish to replace me?

THOMAS PETERS: It is for the people to decide.

JOHN CLARKSON: Then perhaps we should ask them. (*Steps forward.*) Who here instructs me to make it clear to the Sierra Leone Company in London that Thomas Peters is to be your leader and that I should withdraw? (*Nobody moves or raises a hand.*) Well?

THOMAS PETERS: (*To ISAAC.*) Isaac?

ISAAC: Can you not lead together with Mr Clarkson?

THOMAS PETERS: With him?

ISAAC: I wish for no further strife. My desire is that we should all discover a way to exist together.

THOMAS PETERS: Clearly the tropical sun has affected your limited reasoning.

ISAAC: Hold your tongue, Thomas Peters!

THOMAS PETERS: Hold my tongue? You dare speak to me in this fashion?

ANNA MARIA: Perhaps you should listen to the harshness of your own words.

ISAAC: (*To THOMAS PETERS.*) My respect for you does not extend to allowing you to address me in whatever fashion you please. David George has never spoken to me in this manner.

JOHN CLARKSON: And so there are none among you who would have me withdraw and be replaced by Thomas Peters?

DAVID GEORGE: Mr Clarkson, there are none among us who would have you withdraw. The deprivations that we have suffered are not of your making, but we do desire some changes to the order of things.

JOHN CLARKSON: And I desire your continued patience for I have promised you the right to choose men to act on your behalf, and my greatest desire is that this should happen. I have written on many occasions to London, but should the men of the Sierra Leone Company continue to ignore my wishes then I shall return to London and petition them directly.

THOMAS PETERS: (*Addresses the SETTLERS.*) And while our 'African Hero' waits for news from London we continue to suffer because of his broken promises.

DAVID GEORGE: Please, Thomas. No more. Not now.

JOHN CLARKSON: And now, if you will excuse me.

(*JOHN CLARKSON walks off without replying to THOMAS PETERS, who stands with DAVID GEORGE. The SETTLERS begin to disperse.*)

DAVID GEORGE: Perhaps we two should talk.

THOMAS PETERS: Talk with you? (*Laughs.*) No, David George, the time for talking is at an end. It is time for action. But I remember you from the field of battle. You are a timid, fearful man. Action is not for you, is it?

PHYLLIS GEORGE: Thomas, I cannot stand by and watch you insult my husband in this way. You are ruining what respect you have gained, and for what?

THOMAS PETERS: Your husband insults himself. He looks like a white man with the company sash hanging about his person like a chain. (*To DAVID GEORGE.*) Look, at you, you are not an African are you?

DAVID GEORGE: I am a man of African origin.

THOMAS PETERS: (*Laughs.*) So this is what you would have us become. (*Mocks.*) 'I am a man of African origin.' Are you ashamed to call yourself an African?

DAVID GEORGE: I am not ashamed of who I am.

THOMAS PETERS: You are a coward, Mr George! You hide behind your bible. You hide behind the white man's promises. You hide behind the white man's council. But you are clever. I told you, I know you! I can smell the desire for power. You do not fool me. (*Laughs.*) But you fool the white man. Nice, dependable Mr George with his Bible and his fine manners. I can smell you, Mr George.

PHYLLIS GEORGE: My husband's reputation is intact, Thomas. Can you say this about yourself?

THOMAS PETERS: In the quest for what is right and just a man cannot trouble himself with 'reputation'!

PHYLLIS GEORGE: Thomas, nobody is listening to you anymore. You begin now to appear foolish.

THOMAS PETERS: Everybody is listening, Mrs George, including the husband who you claim I insult. The truth is, nobody is speaking. This is the pity. Nobody is speaking out. Even Isaac has fallen under your husband's cowardly spell.

PHYLLIS GEORGE: I am sorry to see a man such as yourself eaten out with bitterness, and I am sure dear Sally would feel the same were she still with us.

THOMAS PETERS: 'Eaten out with bitterness'? No, Mrs George. Still fired with determination, and not bitter. Not yet.

(*PHYLLIS GEORGE and THOMAS PETERS stare at each other.*)

SCENE FOURTEEN

It is night and JOHN CLARKSON sits behind his desk. ALEXANDER FALCONBRIDGE paces somewhat unsteadily in front of him. It is clear that FALCONBRIDGE has been drinking and he remains distressed. JOHN CLARKSON has been interrupted while completing his journal.

JOHN CLARKSON: Mr Falconbridge, should you wish to return to England then I shall not stand in your way.

FALCONBRIDGE: What are you doing, Mr Clarkson? Has this man Peters finally corrupted your reason?

JOHN CLARKSON: Peters is no concern of mine. I am simply trying to run the colony along principles that I believe we promised the blacks.

FALCONBRIDGE: 'We' promised the blacks?

JOHN CLARKSON: The company refuses to answer my requests that the blacks be treated as equals. My conscience therefore dictates that we must simply create such a society.

(*Across the stage we see a WHITE MAN having his shirt removed and then being strapped to a pole. A BLACK MAN steps forward and begins to whip the WHITE MAN.*)

FALCONBRIDGE: (*Laughs.*) No sir, no sir. You court disaster by insisting that blacks and women be allowed to vote. And it is pure folly to allow black to punish white. The Sierra Leone Company has no interest in this utopia of yours. Your 'rules' go against human nature and decency and I want no part of such a society. None!

JOHN CLARKSON: Then, sir, you must leave, for my patience with the Sierra Leone Company has almost run its course.

FALCONBRIDGE: You turn civilization on its head, but for what?

JOHN CLARKSON: For the sake of justice, Mr Falconbridge. Justice and order. The Sierra Leone Company has established a commercial venture replete with extravagance, idleness, quarrelling, waste, irregular accounting, insubordination and a lack of Christian virtue. I can no longer stand by and tolerate this state of affairs. There will be reforms!

FALCONBRIDGE: (*Laughs.*) Your 'reforms' are merely a prelude to disaster. Your blacks have no real love for you.

JOHN CLARKSON: I do not crave their affection.

FALCONBRIDGE: You feel obligated to them?

JOHN CLARKSON: Of course I am obligated to them! I gave them my word!

(*Across the stage the WHITE MAN is untied from the pole and dragged offstage, his punishment complete.*)

FALCONBRIDGE: Have I treated you ill, sir?

JOHN CLARKSON: You have carried out your duties to the best of your abilities, although your abilities have often been affected by your fondness for the grape.

FALCONBRIDGE: There is little reason for you to mock my suffering at this terminus of my life.

JOHN CLARKSON: You are correct, sir. I apologize, I was merely attempting to furnish you with an answer to your question.

FALCONBRIDGE: Should I be fortunate enough to survive a passage to England, how would you have me report your achievements?

JOHN CLARKSON: The truth, Mr Falconbridge. That is all. For many years this second son from Wisbech in Cambridgeshire, has lived in the shadow of his brother,

Thomas, who is indisputably a great man. But I do not compete with my brother for glory, I merely work with him for justice. Tell them this. And remind them that a man should always honour his promises to other men, black or white, for to fail to do so is to cast dishonour upon us all.

FALCONBRIDGE: Sir, on the one side you hold off the self-righteous black anger of those such as the scoundrel, Peters, and on the other side you try to protect this place from what you perceive to be the irregularity of the company. You possess strength that I do not have Mr Clarkson, but eventually you too will tire of this trial. I shall take my leave for England. There is nothing left for me here.

JOHN CLARKSON: I am sorry about the situation with your wife.

FALCONBRIDGE: I imagined that my misfortune might have caused you joy. After all, you seem content to allow blacks to do our duty.

JOHN CLARKSON: I realize it must be painful for you.

FALCONBRIDGE: You have no idea, Mr Clarkson. I cannot stay here.

JOHN CLARKSON: I wish you a safe journey.

(*ALEXANDER FALCONBRIDGE begins to move off, then stops.*)

FALCONBRIDGE: Tell me, Mr Clarkson. Do you intend to be the last surviving white man in these parts? Is this your ambition?

JOHN CLARKSON: There are four or five men who seem content to stay here with me.

FALCONBRIDGE: But none coming out to join you. As a medical man, I can assure you that those who remain will soon be leaving for another world.

JOHN CLARKSON: If necessary, I am prepared to be the last white man in this part of Africa.

FALCONBRIDGE: I see. (*Pause.*) I am sorry, Mr Clarkson. Sorry for you and sorry for your family.

(*ALEXANDER FALCONBRIDGE departs leaving JOHN CLARKSON alone. The skies open and it begins to rain. Hard, torrential tropical rain that beats against an iron roof. A frail-looking THOMAS PETERS is led into a courtroom with his hands tied in front of him. JOHN CLARKSON takes a seat on the bench and gathered all about are BLACKS and WHITES who are there to observe the proceedings.*)

JOHN CLARKSON: Mr Thomas Peters. You stand before this court accused by persons unknown of having stolen the property of one who has recently deceased. This is a most serious matter for no society can tolerate thieves yet expect to function with any moral authority. How do you answer the charges?

THOMAS PETERS: Charges brought against me by persons unknown concerning one who is already deceased? Surely justice has already been betrayed.

JOHN CLARKSON: I have examined the evidence myself, Mr Peters, and it would appear that you have indeed taken property that does not belong to you. (*THOMAS PETERS begins to cough violently.*) Are you in need of assistance, Mr Peters?

THOMAS PETERS: I took property that is rightfully my own as payment for a debt that had been incurred in Nova Scotia. I have nothing to hide for I have done no wrong.

JOHN CLARKSON: So you do not deny that you took the property?

THOMAS PETERS: Of course I took it. I settled a debt which had travelled the ocean, but should the widow be suffering hardships as a result of my actions then I am willing to give back the property to the widow.

JOHN CLARKSON: But the crime has already been committed.

THOMAS PETERS: Crime? What have you done to discipline those whites who take from the company stores, while we blacks suffer the pain of hunger?

JOHN CLARKSON: I have ordered the punishment of black and white without regard to colour, that much you cannot deny.

THOMAS PETERS: You order one white man to be beaten and now you are our saviour?

JOHN CLARKSON: Your impudence is of no concern to me.

THOMAS PETERS: My impudence? Is it wrong of me to resist allegiance to your self-appointed rule over my people.

JOHN CLARKSON: Your people?

THOMAS PETERS: Yes, my people.

JOHN CLARKSON: I think, Mr Peters, that it is already apparent that your people do not recognize you as the leader you imagine yourself to be.

THOMAS PETERS: We shall see, Mr Clarkson. But in the meantime, I refuse to be spoken down to by a white man on African soil.

JOHN CLARKSON: And to you that is all I am? A white man.

THOMAS PETERS: I hope that your God will have some mercy on your soul, and the souls of your colleagues.

JOHN CLARKSON: You are threatening me.

THOMAS PETERS: For over one year you have ruled over us like a small king, but enough Mr Clarkson. Enough!

JOHN CLARKSON: I find you guilty, Mr Peters, of theft and you shall be punished accordingly.

THOMAS PETERS: (*Laughs.*) You cannot punish me, Mr Clarkson, for I already have the victory. These men before you love neither you, Mr Clarkson, nor the Christian minister, Mr George. They love freedom, and they know that true freedom must be taken.

JOHN CLARKSON: Remove him!

THOMAS PETERS: Freedom is never given, Mr Clarkson! It is always taken from people who can no longer hold on to their privilege. It must be taken!

(*A defiant THOMAS PETERS begins to cough violently as he is led away. ANNA MARIA FALCONBRIDGE approaches with ISAAC. JOHN CLARKSON gets to his feet.*)

ANNA MARIA: Mr Clarkson, might I speak with you?

JOHN CLARKSON: Of course, Mrs Falconbridge.

ANNA MARIA: My husband is ailing and planning to return to England. Whether he recovers or not our marriage is no more.

JOHN CLARKSON: So I understand. I am sorry.

ANNA MARIA: I wish for a licence to remarry.

JOHN CLARKSON: To remarry?

ANNA MARIA: To Isaac. (*Pause.*) Surely you are not surprised, Mr Clarkson.

JOHN CLARKSON: Well I was aware of some affection between the two of you, but it had not occurred to me that marriage was a possibility.

ISAAC: And does this prospect concern you?

JOHN CLARKSON: Concern me?

ANNA MARIA: (*Laughs.*) Mr Clarkson, Isaac has brought joy into my life. Do you object to marriage? Or is it *our* union that you find difficult to imagine?

JOHN CLARKSON: If marriage is what you eventually desire, then it is not my place to pass judgement.

ANNA MARIA: Thank you. I shall, of course, keep you apprised of Mr Falconbridge's condition.

(*ISAAC and ANNA MARIA begin to move off, and then they stop. ANNA MARIA takes a step back towards JOHN CLARKSON.*)

Forgive me, Mr Clarkson, but is there not somebody for you in England?

JOHN CLARKSON: Somebody for me?

ANNA MARIA: A fiancée? A sweetheart perhaps?

JOHN CLARKSON: I recently received news that she is married. (*Pause.*) She is a friend, the connection is no more than this. (*Pause.*) Eliza is wed to a Mr Prowse of Wicken Park in Northamptonshire. I am led to believe that he is a fine man of substantial means.

ANNA MARIA: Mr Clarkson.

JOHN CLARKSON: Mrs Falconbridge.

ANNA MARIA: You deserve a measure of happiness. Perhaps you too, like my husband, might consider returning to England.

JOHN CLARKSON: To England?

ANNA MARIA: If only for a few months. Fresh air. Recuperation of the heart and mind. Particularly of the heart. Surely you miss your home?

JOHN CLARKSON: Mrs Falconbridge I miss my life on the sea. I do not miss the coffee houses of The Strand or Fleet Street. Neither do I miss the bustle of Drury Lane. I miss the sea and my old naval life. I miss the obedience, discipline and order of His Majesty's Navy, but perhaps this career is behind me now, I do not know. Back in England there is, beyond my distinguished brother, nobody who mourns my absence. I have lost sight of England.

ANNA MARIA: Is this place now your home?

JOHN CLARKSON: Until the company allows these blacks the right to determine the course of their own lives then this place will be home to none, black or white.

ANNA MARIA: Which is why you must return to England. To your home.

JOHN CLARKSON: I have no desire to abandon them.

ANNA MARIA: You wish to remain in Africa?

JOHN CLARKSON: My destiny is tied to these men.

ANNA MARIA: I understand, Mr Clarkson. But sometimes one must think of one's own happiness. (*Pause.*) Mr Clarkson, I believe you deserve to be happy.

(*ANNA MARIA walks off with ISAAC and leaves JOHN CLARKSON alone. He turns and approaches an ill-looking THOMAS PETERS in his cell. A WHITE JAILER guards the prisoner.*)

JOHN CLARKSON: (*To JAILER.*) You may leave us alone.

JAILER: But, Mr Clarkson, sir.

JOHN CLARKSON: Mr Peters and I know each other.

THOMAS PETERS: You are predictable, Mr Clarkson.

JOHN CLARKSON: You were expecting me?

THOMAS PETERS: (*Laughs.*) Where is your olive branch?

JOHN CLARKSON: (*To JAILER.*) Please wait outside. (*The reluctant JAILER moves off.*) Mr Peters, you are ill. Can I send Mr Falconbridge to you?

THOMAS PETERS: The man should be in charge of a tavern. He is no doctor.

JOHN CLARKSON: He is all we have.

THOMAS PETERS: I shall recover my strength without recourse to your white medicine.

JOHN CLARKSON: I have written many times to the company in London asking for another doctor to be sent out, along with medical supplies. (*Pause.*) Sometimes I imagine they must have forgotten us.

THOMAS PETERS: They have not forgotten. They simply do not share your ideals, Mr Clarkson. Without their help you are lost, and they know this.

JOHN CLARKSON: How then must I go forward with my life?

THOMAS PETERS: You ask me how you should conduct your life?

JOHN CLARKSON: I am in conversation with myself.

THOMAS PETERS: Then I beg you take your conversation elsewhere and allow me some peace and quiet.

JOHN CLARKSON: You wish me to leave?

THOMAS PETERS: If I am not a part of your conversation then you have no business here.

JOHN CLARKSON: There is no necessity for you to fester in this cell. Simply come and serve on the council. Show that you are willing to invest your faith in the future of the province.

THOMAS PETERS: A demonstration of my faith in the province, or my faith in you?

JOHN CLARKSON: You choose to live apart from everybody, black and white, yet you also desire to lead. I do not understand.

THOMAS PETERS: I exercise vigilance, Mr Clarkson. I have learned that I must wait, but I must wait in a place where I can see my people and they can see me.

JOHN CLARKSON: And can they see you in this prison cell, Mr Peters?

THOMAS PETERS: (*Laughs, then coughs hard.*) They can see me.

JOHN CLARKSON: Do you seek separation from the white race?

THOMAS PETERS: In some circumstances, separation is emancipation.

(*THOMAS PETERS and JOHN CLARKSON stare at each other.*)

JOHN CLARKSON: Why steal from another man?

THOMAS PETERS: There are real thieves in your community, Mr Clarkson. White thieves.

JOHN CLARKSON: To my mind it is morally odious to take from another man that which is not yours.

THOMAS PETERS: I am not a thief, Mr Clarkson.

JOHN CLARKSON: And if we pardon you, and you join the council, would this not be powerful evidence of your innocence?

THOMAS PETERS: Or evidence of my desperation? By imprisoning me, Mr Clarkson, you damage your own situation.

JOHN CLARKSON: You are entitled to your own opinion.

THOMAS PETERS: You must leave now.

JOHN CLARKSON: I must leave?

THOMAS PETERS: Is there more that you wish to discuss?

(*JOHN CLARKSON moves off slightly. The JAILER enters.*)

JOHN CLARKSON: You are a stubborn man, Mr Peters.

THOMAS PETERS: Yet you followed me to Nova Scotia.

JOHN CLARKSON: I followed you?

THOMAS PETERS: You followed me, Mr Clarkson. (*Laughs.*) Have you forgotten?

(*They stare at each other. The JAILER seems anxious, but he says nothing.*)

SCENE FIFTEEN

Sombre church bells ring out and in the half-light we see MEN carrying a coffin that is then lowered into the ground. As the lights come up it is a bright, warm afternoon, and a picnic is in full progress. Clearly a departure is being heralded. JOHN CLARKSON, dressed in naval uniform, stands and receives a line of SETTLERS, who are presenting him with offerings for his journey. Yams, papaya, onion, chickens and eggs. ISAAC stands with him. ANNA MARIA stands to ISAAC's side.

JOHN CLARKSON: Thank you. Thank you very much.

SETTLER 1: God bless you Mr Clarkson.

SETTLER 2: Safe journey, master.

JOHN CLARKSON: Thank you, Dolly.

(*DAVID GEORGE enters with PHYLLIS GEORGE. He is dressed like an Englishman and clearly about to undertake a journey.*)

DAVID GEORGE: Thank you for allowing us to bury Thomas Peters with dignity.

JOHN CLARKSON: Mr Peters had his virtues.

ISAAC: For many of us, he spoke the truth.

JOHN CLARKSON: Mr Peters could try the patience of a saint, but I suppose some part of me admired his persistence.

ISAAC: Mr Peters wanted to be master in his own home. That is all. And you, Mr Clarkson, now you are leaving for your home.

JOHN CLARKSON: I shall restate my case to the Sierra Leone Company, but this time in person.

DAVID GEORGE: Mr Clarkson intends to return to us.

JOHN CLARKSON: Indeed I do, but if the company wishes to dispatch a replacement, then they are at liberty to do so.

ISAAC: (*To JOHN CLARKSON.*) Mr Peters was trying to tell you that we are free men who have fought for the British and paid for our land and freedom with blood.

ANNA MARIA: Isaac, please. Mr Clarkson is aware of your situation.

JOHN CLARKSON: I have done my best at all times.

ANNA MARIA: Nobody disputes this fact.

JOHN CLARKSON: (*To ISAAC.*) How is a man supposed to strike a balance between benevolence and authority? Do you have any notion, Isaac?

ISAAC: I am not a leader of men. (*To DAVID GEORGE.*) Are you, Mr George?

DAVID GEORGE: (*To ISAAC.*) Perhaps you might lend my wife assistance in my absence?

ANNA MARIA: We will be happy to do so.

DAVID GEORGE: (*To JOHN CLARKSON.*) I am ready. (*He turns to the assembled SETTLERS.*) I am to journey to England with Mr Clarkson, who promises to represent our concerns to the Sierra Leone Company. (*Turns towards JOHN CLARKSON.*) Mr Clarkson, you were handed a difficult command by your colleagues in London and you have conducted yourself with some dignity. But time has passed and Mr Peters died asking questions that still need to be answered. Why can we not be trusted to govern ourselves without any interference from London? Why can we not be trusted to establish our own laws? I shall travel with you and ask these questions directly in London. (*To the SETTLERS.*) And I shall return with answers. (*They cheer.*) I ask all of you to remain patient during my absence. Either I alone shall return, or I shall return in company with Mr Clarkson, but I *will* bring answers. That much I promise to all of you. We *shall* rule ourselves and be answerable to none beyond those that we elect and God the almighty.

(*Hats are tossed in the air and handkerchiefs waved as JOHN CLARKSON and DAVID GEORGE begin to move off in the direction of the ship with the CROWD following them. The two men board the ship and stand on deck as it moves away from shore. The CROWD begins to recede from view.*)

JOHN CLARKSON: David.

DAVID GEORGE: Mr George.

JOHN CLARKSON: Mr George?

DAVID GEORGE: We owe ultimate allegiance to none but the Lord. Do you believe this, Mr Clarkson?

JOHN CLARKSON: I am a Christian.

DAVID GEORGE: No man owes allegiance to commerce, but a slave. And slaves come in all shades, Mr Clarkson.

JOHN CLARKSON: I understand.

DAVID GEORGE: You have served us well, Mr Clarkson, but now you must return home.

JOHN CLARKSON: Mr George, are you ready to remove me with force?

DAVID GEORGE: I do not think that will be necessary, do you?

JOHN CLARKSON: I believe some intemperate part of you is Thomas Peters.

DAVID GEORGE: (*Laughs.*) Some part of us all is Thomas Peters.

JOHN CLARKSON: Do you truly believe this?

DAVID GEORGE: Mr Clarkson, should you lose your freedom perhaps then, and only then, will you truly understand.

JOHN CLARKSON: Are you familiar with Doctor Johnson's dictionary?

DAVID GEORGE: I know of its existence.

JOHN CLARKSON: During my naval years I kept a copy with me and endeavoured to learn a new word each day. The dictionary gives us structure and stability. Order.

DAVID GEORGE: These are words, Mr Clarkson. Mere words. And each day men make slaves of words. (*Pause.*) Rest, Mr Clarkson. The sun has set on your labours. We must complete the journey without you.

JOHN CLARKSON: And how will you speak of me in London?

DAVID GEORGE: I have a petition from my people expressly stating your courage and their gratitude.

JOHN CLARKSON: But we have already established that these are words, Mr George. How shall *you* speak of me?

DAVID GEORGE: Rest, Mr Clarkson. (*He points.*) Over there, on the horizon, a new day shall soon rise up out of the ocean. To whom does this new day belong? To you?

JOHN CLARKSON: To us?

(*DAVID GEORGE looks at JOHN CLARKSON and then they both watch as the sun rises in the east and a new day begins.*)

END OF PLAY